TESSA EVELEGH

Photography by Laura Edwards

ESSENTIAL *Sewing*

A manual for learning to sew with 25 projects

Fons&Porter

CONTENTS

34 Tunic

40 Pajama pants

68 Summer dress

76 Laundry bag

106 Tie pillow

110 Cook's apron

140 Camisole

146 Boyfriend shirt

176 Tote bag

184 Blouse with collar

46 Button-back blouse

52 Floor cushion

56 Edge-to-edge jacket

62 Pencil skirt

82 Basic curtains

88 Circular skirt

94 Tea dress

100 Girl's dress

116 Prom dress

122 Window panel

126 Hacking jacket

134 Bow tie

154 Patchwork throw

158 Roman shade

164 Basic dress

170 Vest

190 Butcher's apron

196 Ruffle pillow

THE JOY OF SEWING

Whether you want to learn to stitch from scratch, dress yourself, or dress your home, you'll find all you need to get yourself started in this book. Like any craft, it takes time to build sewing skills. Just like learning to drive, while the basics don't take long to master, you do need practice time to become really proficient. This doesn't mean you can't produce something lovely right from the start, and that is what this book is all about.

Designed to take you step by step through all the basics skills, this book gives essential information on how to decipher paper patterns, lists the equipment needed, and teaches how to choose fabrics like a professional. But the main element of the book is a menu of fabulous projects—both fashion and household—designed with the beginner in mind.

The CD-rom at the back of the book includes tiled, PDF versions of all the pattern pieces. You can print and assemble the sheets following the instructions (provided as a PDF on the CD), or by photocopying and enlarging the pattern pieces printed in the book.

STARTING TO SEW

STOCKING THE SEWING BOX

A well-stocked sewing box is essential, whether you are sewing by hand or by machine. You don't need complicated tools or equipment and most of what you need to start sewing may already be familiar.

Needles

Using the right needles for the job will make your work infinitely easier and quicker. Needles should be kept in a needlebook as they can easily become blunt when left to rattle around in a box.

SHARPS are all-purpose needles with easy-to-thread eyes. Available in twelve sizes, the most useful are sizes 6 to 9.
BETWEENS are the short, fine needles with small eyes used by quilters to quickly work tiny, even stitches. These come in 12 sizes, but as quilting requires a fine needle, sizes 8 to 12 are most useful.
CREWEL or embroidery needles are long and have oval eyes to make quick work of threading strands of embroidery floss. The larger sizes 3 to 6 are the most useful as they are easiest to thread.
TAPESTRY and cross-stitch needles are for use on needlepoint canvas and evenweave fabrics. They have blunt tips so they can pass between the fabric threads without piercing them.
DARNING needles are long, sturdy, large eyed, and blunt tipped. This combination makes it easy to thread them with wool and to easily weave in and out of wool strands.
BEADING needles are long and very fine, so they can easily slip through small bead holes.
UPHOLSTERY demands its own particular needles that are strong and sturdy. They include some that are very long for buttoning work and curved ones to slipstitch three-dimensional cushions.
MACHINE needles come in four point styles: sharps for general sewing, light ballpoint for fine jerseys, medium ballpoint for heavier-weight jerseys, and wedge-point for plastic-coated fabrics, felt, and leather. They range in sizes from 9/65 for silks to 18/110 for canvas. 14/90 is the size for medium-weight fabrics. Always use the correct point style and size, otherwise the needle may break and damage the machine.

Thimble

Available in metal, plastic, or silicon, a thimble protects the end of the finger used to push the needle through when hand sewing.

Needle threader

A fine wire loop that can be pushed through the eye of a needle for easy threading.

Pins

Choose the right pins for the job to speed up the project. Keep them in a pincushion to keep them sharp.

HOUSEHOLD pins are robust general-purpose pins.
DRESSMAKER'S pins are finer so they don't mark fabric.
BRIDAL or lace pins are the finest of all.
GLASS- or pearl-headed pins are longer than general household pins, easier on the fingertips, and easier to see (therefore also easier remove when you need to).
QUILTER'S pins are extra-long glass-headed pins.

Bodkin

A professional tool used for threading through casings. There are two types: the first is a large blunt needle with a large eye for elastic; the second is a "pinch" type and clasps ribbon ready to thread through a casing.

Safety pins

Among others things, safety pins can be used as improvised bodkins to thread elastic through casings.

Measuring tools

Just like carpenters, dressmakers are best advised to measure twice (at least) and cut once. The more accurately the pieces are measured, the more accurately they're likely to be cut and the better end result.

TAILOR'S MEASURING TAPE

This soft cloth tape is coated (usually with plastic) to prevent it from stretching. Perfect for taking fabric-piece and body measurements during dressmaking.

STEEL TAPE

You'll need this for curtain making—both to measure up windows and the lengths of fabric during construction.

RULERS

Choose a stable ruler made of steel or plastic that is at least 12–18" (30–45 cm) long. This is handy for accurate measurements, and drawing straight lines. A yardstick (meterstick) is useful for measuring hems.

SEWING GAUGE

This is a handy ruler about 6" (15 cm) long that incorporates a slider/marker for accurate measurement of hems and small pieces such as collars and cuffs. It also incorporates a point to help with turning through collars.

Marking tools

Once you've cut out the fabric, you'll need to accurately transfer the markings from the paper or tissue pattern to all the layers of material. You'll also sometimes need to mark adjustments to garments during the making process. There are several tools for doing this, ranging from traditional tailor's chalk and tailor's tacks to water-soluble and heat-transfer pencils.

TAILOR'S CHALK

A fine chalk that readily marks fabric yet easily brushes off. Available in several colors, it comes in traditional squares or rounded triangular shapes, or in a self-sharpening container. It is most useful for making adjustments as it is difficult to accurately transfer markings from the paper pattern pieces using chalk.

WATER-SOLUBLE DRESSMAKER'S PENCILS

These pencils are used for making marks on fabric that can then be removed by water. Push the tip of the pencil through the pattern piece, marking one layer at a time.

HEAT TRANSFER PENCILS

Transfer markings easily by tracing them onto paper with these pencils, then ironing them onto the fabric.

DRESSMAKER'S CARBON AND TRACING WHEEL

A piece of carbon is placed between the pattern piece and every layer of fabric. The tracing wheel transfers the marks from the pattern onto all layers.

Cutting tools

Clean, accurate cuts are essential for the speed and success of any sewing project. When it comes to cutting tools, it is worth investing in the best. Quality scissors not only have sharp blades that have been properly ground, but they have been ergonomically designed. This means the tool is comfortable in the hand and the weight is appropriate for the job.

DRESSMAKER'S SHEARS

These shears must be very sharp, with blades at least 8" (20 cm) long and handles that bend upward so the fabric stays flat on the cutting surface. The best quality shears are heavy in the hand—this helps to steady them as you cut. Try them out. Most of your hand should fit in the lower handle and your thumb should feel comfortable in the top one. Save your dressmaker's shears just for fabrics—other materials can blunt them.

SPRING-LOADED SHEARS

These are not as heavy as traditional shears and have a spring that opens the blades so all you have to do is squeeze to cut. Possibly easier to handle if you have arthritis, but try them first. Not as long lasting as traditional shears as the spring can lose its effectiveness.

HOUSEHOLD SCISSORS

Use these to cut out the paper patterns to save blunting your fabric shears.

PINKING SHEARS

The zigzag blades of these cut a decorative edge while reducing the fraying (unraveling) of the fabric. This is one of the quickest and easiest ways to finish seams. Pinking shears can also be used to cut a decorative edge on fabrics that don't fray, such as felt.

EMBROIDERY SCISSORS

Small and lightweight, use these to accurately snip threads and embroidery threads.

THREAD CLIPS

This spring-loaded tool fits neatly in your hand with a thumb-hole on the top. Small, lightweight, and comfortable to use, it's great for quickly and neatly snipping sewing and embroidery threads.

ROTARY CUTTER

Looking much like a pizza cutter, rotary cutters are used mainly by quilters, to cut several layers of fabric at once. They need to be used in conjunction with a quilter's ruler on a cutting mat, both of which are marked out with lines and angles to help quilters cut accurate squares and triangles.

SEAM RIPPER

A small fork-like tool that makes quick work of undoing any mistakes.

 Try this…

If you can't find a sewing box you like, check out a DIY store. Toolboxes with plenty of compartments can be ideal for storing your sewing needs. Plastic toolboxes are the best choice as they are lightweight and therefore easy to carry.

TOOLS OF THE TRADE

As with any job, you need the right tools. Without them, your sewing will take longer, be more difficult, and the finish will not be as professional. Thankfully, it's not overly expensive to set yourself up with a basic sewing kit. Here's what you need.

The sewing machine

The sewing machine is the biggest investment. It is also the most essential, so, if you're a complete beginner, before rushing out and buying one, you might prefer to start off by borrowing a machine, or trying a workshop that provides them. Having said that, basic home sewing machines are reasonably priced and bearing in mind the jobs you will be able to use them for over the years, they are worth the investment. Give yourself time when choosing. Make sure you can have a test run before buying, and think carefully about what you really need. It is easy to be persuaded by an expensive all-singing, all-dancing computerized machine that offers fancy embroidery options when most of the time, you'll only be using the straight stitch, zigzag stitch, a decent buttonholer, and possibly a few standard "fancy" stitches.

Machine accessories

The simplest modern machine comes with a basic toolkit, including:

STANDARD ATTACHMENTS
An all-purpose foot for general sewing, a zipper foot, and a blind hem foot. There are often two spool holders of different sizes to hold the spool of thread in position on the top of the machine as you sew. You'll also get spare bobbins, needles, and a seam ripper. For sewing machine maintenance, you'll get a screwdriver and cleaning tool.

SPECIAL ATTACHMENTS
Most people find the basic toolkit enough for most jobs, though an invisible zipper foot would be a useful extra buy. As you become more experienced, you may want to invest in a binder for neatly applying bias binding, rufflers, tuckers, and endless others. When buying attachments, make sure that they are the correct ones for your machine—each manufacturer's are slightly different.

The overlocker

This is an expensive separate professional machine used to trim and finish off the edges of the seams in a single action. Because it cuts the fabrics as it sews, you need to be a confident machinist before attempting to use an overlocker. There are many alternative ways to finish seam edges (pages 214–215) so an overlocker is not essential. However, most proficient sewers love the finish an overlocker brings to their work.

Whatever machine you have, there will be times when it just doesn't seem to behave. Like with a car or computer, you'll become increasingly proficient with your sewing machine as you use it. As each model is different, get to know your own by studying the manual. Here are some tips to get you going and troubleshooting hints for when you get exasperated.

Before you start

Start by selecting the right stitch length for the fabric. Generally you'll need shorter stitches for fine fabrics and longer ones if you're stitching heavier fabrics. Cut two squares of fabric to represent a seam of the garment you plan to make. Now work a line of stitches on the bias. The stitches should look even with no loops on the front or the back of the fabric. Pull the fabric to check the stitches don't break. Now look closer at the stitches. The top thread and bottom (bobbin) thread should lock together where the fabric thicknesses meet. If the bobbin thread is being pulled to the top surface or the top thread down to the under layer, the tension may need adjusting. However, a lot of "tension" problems can actually be traced to threading basics. So first, try these steps.

USE THE RIGHT THREAD IN THE BOBBIN
Wind the bobbin from the spool of thread you are using for the project—then the top and bottom thread will work in harmony and will not fight each other.

REMOVE ANY STRAY THREADS
Clear out any threads under the throat plate or between the tension disks.

CHECK THE BOBBIN
Is the thread running freely? If not, remove the bobbin from its housing and unreel any jammed thread. Then re-wind it slowly following the manufacturer's instructions to ensure it's evenly wound.

CHECK THE NEEDLE
Ensure you're using the correct needle. Silks and chiffons require finer needles. Change the needle if necessary.

RE-THREAD THE MACHINE
Make sure the spool holder is the right size for the spool. Now re-thread, ensuring the thread passes freely through all the thread guides and the presser foot is down before threading the needle. Re-try the stitch sample. If there's still a problem, make a small adjustment to the tension.

ADJUST THE TENSION
Machines are tension-corrected before being sold, so the tension dial is most likely to be set at 4. If you generally sew on a tension other than 4, take the machine back to the supplier to re-set the tension. The only adjustment to the tension you may need to make will probably be to allow for an especially fine or particularly heavy fabric. If your machine is currently set at 4 and, after all the above checks, your top stitches still look loopy, turn the dial to a higher number; if the underside stitches look loopy, you'll need to turn the dial to a lower number. If you're using a more regular fabric for your next project, you should expect to readjust the tension dial back to 4.

Troubleshooting

NEEDLE JAMS
Check the needle hasn't worked loose in the shaft. Re-fit it and ensure the screw is properly tightened. Check you're using the right foot—if you switch to zigzag stitch, change the foot to one that allows for a swing needle.

NEEDLE BREAKS
It might have hit metal—a pin or zipper teeth. It might also have worked loose in the shaft and broken because it hit the throat plate. Replace the needle.

STITCHES WON'T FORM
Check that there is thread on the bobbin and that the machine is properly threaded.

BOTTOM THREAD BREAKS
Remove the bobbin, clean out any threads from the bobbin housing. Re-wind the bobbin and re-thread the machine.

TOP THREAD BREAKS
Check you're using the right needle for the fabric. If not, replace the needle, then re-thread the machine.

Commercial patterns are the sewing equivalent of cooking recipes. The envelope and its contents give you all the information needed to make the garment. It's a blueprint, if you like, because no two handmade garments will ever be identical. You can add your own flair with the choice of fabrics, trimmings, and buttons, and even adapt the pattern a little if you like. The symbols and diagrams might look intimidating, but once you start using them, you'll find them as easy to follow as any recipe.

Start at the back

Once you've chosen the design you like, decipher the back of the pattern packet. You'll find technical sketches of the back views, showing the positions of any seams, fastenings, and trimmings. The rest of the back of the envelope is given over to all the information you need to buy the materials. Here's what to expect:

🔍 *Body measurements for all the standard sizes included in the pattern, given in both inches and centimeters.*

🔍 *Garment measurements showing the exact finished size of the clothing once made. This allows for ease and movement.*

🔍 *Fabric requirements for each size, including the amounts needed for different fabric widths. A suitable fabrics list gives fiber options.*

🔍 *Notions list of all you'll need to complete the garment: zippers, buttons, snaps, ribbon, elastic, etc.*

Next look inside

Inside the envelope, you'll find an instruction sheet and full-sized tissue pattern pieces. Most patterns are multi-sized so there may be a different cutting line (solid, dotted, or dashed) to follow for each size. The pattern pieces may also be marked with symbols that relate to the instructions. Here are the most common symbols:

Straight of grain—place this line parallel to the selvage of the fabric to ensure the piece is cut in line with the grain

Foldline—place this edge on the foldline of the fabric in order to cut a perfectly symmetrical piece

Adjustment—lengthen or shorten a piece between these lines

Notches—match fabric pieces by aligning the notches

Dots—these indicate, for example, the beginning and end of gathers or easing stitches

Darts—theses indicate where contour shaping is to be added

Buttonhole—these indicate where a buttonhole is to be sewn

Prepare the pattern pieces

Most pattern packs contain several variations of one or more designs. Whichever version of a particular design you choose to make, you will need only some of the numbered tissue pattern pieces. There will be a list of which pieces are needed for each option, so start by carefully cutting them out along the cutting line given for your size using paper or household scissors. Finally, iron each tissue pattern piece using a cool iron to remove any folds or creases.

Prepare the fabric

Before you begin to sew, ensure that your fabric has been pre-shrunk, otherwise the final made-up garment may become distorted the first time you launder it. When you buy your fabric, check the care label on the roll or bolt. If it's a dry clean material then the fabric should remain stable so there is no need to launder it. If not, wash, dry, and iron the fabric.

Next, make sure the fabric is lying straight across the cross grain—the horizontal threads of the fabric should run at right angles to the woven side edge, or selvage. The best way to do this is to pull out a single thread across the width of the fabric to give a straight line to cut along. You won't be able to do this with jacquards because of the way they are woven. For these, you'll need to draw a straight line across the grain. Do this by lining up a gridded quilter's ruler or drafting triangle against the selvage so you can draw a line at right angles to it across the fabric width. Cut along the marked line to ensure that the fabric edge is perfectly straight.

It is essential the threads of the fabric are straight and the pattern pieces are cut on the correct grain, with the straight of grain arrows parallel to the direction of the woven threads, otherwise the fabric—and consquently the finished garment—may not hang correctly.

Take the measurements

While couturiers and theater costumiers make each garment to fit a specific client or actor, ready-to-wear fashion comes in off-the-peg sizes, but few of us are off-the-peg people. If we're lucky, we might have the requisite off-the-peg bust, waist, and hip measurement, but we might also have a longer back, wider shoulders, and longer or shorter arms or legs. Making your own garments has the huge advantage of allowing for pattern adjustments before we even begin to cut out the fabric.

Professional tailors take endless measurements and make infinite adjustments, but for the home dressmaker, even a few measurements can make all the difference to a garment's fit and fall. The most useful measurements to take are:

✂ *Full bust*—around the bust at its fullest point
✂ *Bust point*—from the shoulder down to the fullest point of the bust
✂ *Waist*—around the narrowest part of the waist
✂ *Back waist*—from the vertebra at the base of the neck to the small of the back
✂ *Hip*—around the hips at the widest part of the abdomen and buttocks
✂ *Sleeve length*—from the shoulder to the wrist via the bent elbow
✂ *Side length*—from the waist to the desired length of the skirt, shorts, or trousers

Adjust the pattern

There are two parallel lines at points of the pattern where it can be adjusted while retaining the basic shape of the piece. If you need to shorten the piece, make a fold between the lines to shorten it by the required amount. If you want to lengthen it, cut between the lines, then use masking tape and a strip of spare paper to elongate the pattern piece.

If you want to make widthwise adjustments, remember that because each pattern piece represents a quarter of your body, you will need to enlarge or reduce it by a quarter of the overall difference between the body measurement (NOT garment measurement) stated on the pattern and your own body measurement. So, if your waist is 1" (2.5 cm) smaller than the body measurement stated on the pattern, you will want to reduce each piece by ¼" (6 mm). If it is a small amount (which it should be if you have a multi-sized pattern), it's probably easiest to take this amount off each side seam.

Lay out the pattern pieces

The instruction sheet inside the pattern envelope will include a layout plan for each garment option, which shows you how to cut out all the necessary pattern pieces from your length of fabric. This cutting guide will be marked with any relevant symbols, such as the straight of grain and foldline for any pieces that must be cut from folded fabric. If you decide to work out your own layout, make sure that you always follow these two markings on the pattern.

NAP AND DIRECTIONAL PATTERNS

If you are using a fabric with a nap (a pile or a weave such as herringbone that runs in one direction), or one with a pattern that goes in one direction, a tartan, for example, or a repeated motif, make sure all the pieces run in the same direction. This may require extra fabric.

CENTERING PATTERNS

A fabric with a large motif pattern repeat will need to be centered on the garment. Sometimes, it is easier to do this on a single layer of fabric so you can make sure each piece is centered accurately. If you do fold the fabric, make sure the fold runs accurately down the center of the motif, or between two motifs.

PINNING

Place the pieces in position on the fabric. Pin any in position on the fold, smoothing the pattern out as you do so. Next, pin along the straight of grain of the other pieces. Measure from the grain line out to the selvage (the finished edges running down each side edge of the fabric) in several places to ensure the pattern piece is lying straight. Pin it in position along the grain line. Now use your hand to smooth out from this line toward the edges of the pattern piece to make sure it is lying flat, then pin in position.

Cut out the fabric pieces

Use dressmaker's shears to cut out the pattern pieces from your fabric, using long clean cuts for a smart finish. Cut out any notches as you come to them.

Make your marks

Once all the fabric pieces are cut out, you need to transfer the markings such as darts, buttons, buttonholes, tuck positions, and dots that mark the positioning of pockets, gathering, and easing, for example. Everything needs to be marked on all the layers of fabric. There are several ways to do this.

USING A TRACING WHEEL AND DRESSMAKER'S CARBON

This is the quickest and easiest method. First, test the carbon (which comes in packs of several colors) on a spare piece of fabric. Choose a color that shows up on your fabric, while being its closest match. Once you're ready to go, place a piece of carbon between the tissue paper pattern piece and each layer of fabric so the transferable side of the carbon marks the wrong side of the fabric. Use double-sided carbon where there are two layers of fabric. Simply run the tracer wheel over the lines you want to mark. Where there's a dot, trace a small cross.

USING MARKER PENS AND PENCILS

These can only mark one layer at a time. Marking the wrong side of the fabric, push the pen or pencil through the tissue to the fabric at points you want to mark. Reposition the tissue on the second layer of fabric and repeat. Draw in lines, such as dart lines using the marker and ruler.

USING TAILOR'S TACKS

The only equipment you need for tailor's tacks is a needle and contrasting thread. Here's how to make them.

✎ *Thread the needle with doubled thread but do not knot the end.*

✎ *Make long very loopy stitches along any lines you want to mark and cut the thread long at the end of the line. For dots, take one small stitch but leave both ends of the threads long.*

✎ *Now snip the loops made by the stitches. You should have a line of long, cut double threads marking, for example, the line of a dart.*

✎ *Remove the tissue pattern. Now lift the top layer of fabric a little and snip the threads between the layers of fabric. Both layers will be left with little tufts of marker threads.*

Part of the thrill and inspiration for sewing-your-own is the treasure trove of fabrics that come in an infinite combination of colors, textures, and patterns. From pretty printed cottons to textured wool tweeds, delicate laces to rich brocades and damasks, there's endless potential for creating something special that expresses your own individual sense of style and flair. Choosing the fabric and trimmings is one of the most important steps in the design process.

Furnishing fabrics

Most of these are more heavyweight than fashion fabrics, as they need to provide plenty of drape for curtains and, more importantly, be able to withstand the constant wear and tear demanded of upholstery. You'll also find sheers in the furnishing fabric department, designed to let light into the room while protecting privacy. They can be made from loose-woven cotton organdy, linen, or fine synthetics. At 60" (150 cm) wide or more, furnishing fabrics are wider than fashion fabrics, designed to deal with large-scale projects.

Fashion fabrics

You'll find these grouped in various different sections within the store—not just by fiber type, but also by pattern. So there may be a cottons section, which is subdivided into plains, printed patterns, and wovens. Most fashion fabrics are 45" (115 cm) wide, though some are 60" (150 cm) wide. This makes a big difference to the amount of fabric you need to buy and most patterns list the quantities required for each width.

Additional fabrics

As well as the main fabrics, there is a wide choice of "supporting" materials, which are used to create extra body and give a more luxurious finish to both garments and curtains.

LINING FABRICS

These come in a rainbow of colors, made from silk-like acetate for garments and cotton sateen for curtains. You can, of course, use any other fabric for lining, though it should generally be lighter weight than the main fabric, supporting rather than changing the shape and drape of the item.

INTERFACING AND INTERLINING

Used to add extra support, structure, and/or warmth interfacings and interlinings are available in a variety of weights. Traditionally, interfacings were stitched in position, although now many can be ironed on.

BATTING

Batting for quiltmaking, padded jackets, and upholstery is available in many thicknesses.

Woven wool patterns

Fabrics are made up of three elements: the fiber, the way in which it is woven and how the pattern is achieved. These three fabrics are all twill-woven wool. Each pattern is built up within the weave by threading up the loom with different colors in a particular order so that the geometric patterns (including the classic dogtooth at the bottom) are created during the weaving process (see opposite page).

MAKING THE RIGHT CHOICE

It's the color and pattern of a fabric that we're initially attracted to, but there are many more considerations before you're ready to make your choice. Is it fit for purpose? How does it drape? If you have already chosen a dressmaking pattern, check the back of the envelope and choose from the suggested list. Home furnishing projects are a little less complicated. If you're making curtains or scatter pillows, any furnishing fabric should work. But for anything that you may sit on, you will need to choose only from labeled upholstery fabric that will be able to stand the wear and tear. Whether you're working on a fashion or soft-furnishing project, run through this checklist to make sure that your choice will work with the design and is of good quality.

UNROLL A LENGTH of the fabric and check the size of the pattern repeat against your chosen design. Large patterns, for example, won't be suitable for dresses made up of several small pieces. Stripes, plaids, one-way patterns, and the way the pile lies on a fabric such as velvet (which is known as nap) can affect the suitability and quantity needed for the design; check the fabric notes on the back of the pattern envelope.

HOLD THE FABRIC up to the light to assess the density of the weave. The looser the weave, the more easily it will fray and you will need to be extra careful when finishing the seams.

CHECK THE QUALITY as generally (but not always) the denser the weave, the better the quality. Some loose-weave sheer fabrics, such as cotton organdy, have been constructed and treated in a particular way to give them a crisp finish with excellent drape that is permanent, even through washing. But beware of choosing a pretty pattern on a loose weave that appears to have more body than you would expect. Many fabrics are treated, or "dressed" for extra body, but this soon washes out.

So how can you gauge quality? Here are clues to help. Feel the weight: is it appropriate for the type of fabric? Cast your eye over a length of the fabric to check for color inconsistencies or flaws within the weave. Look at the printed pattern (if there is one): is it parallel with the edges? Do stripes run straight or are they running slightly off the straight of grain?

TRY OUT THE DRAPE to assess if the fabric is soft and flowing or whether it has plenty of body? Hold the fabric in the way it will drape when made up. For example, if it's going to be gathered, gather some up in your hand to see how it falls.

STRETCH IT with the grain and across the bias to check how much it gives and whether or not that works with your chosen design.

ASSESS ITS WEARABILITY and laundry requirements by checking the care label. Every roll of fabric should have a care label and a fiber content list. Crush the fabric in your hand to see how it creases and how readily it springs back.

Hard workers

The honest weaves and unpretentious designs of traditional heavy-duty cotton utility fabrics have become very popular in recent years, but this time as furnishing fabrics. The top fabric is a ticking, traditionally twill-woven with dark blue or charcoal stripes and used to make pillows. Naturally robust enough even for upholstery, it has been resurrected as a smart furnishing fabric in a wide range of colors and stripe variations. The lower two fabrics are variations on traditional plain-weave floursack materials (see opposite page).

Natural fibers

Before scientific advances saw the invention of synthetic fibers, all fabrics were made from natural fibers. These are generally still seen as more desirable than synthetic: they all have a subtle natural sheen and are more comfortable against the skin. Most (although not all) are easier to sew as they are inclined to be less slippery. Since the introduction of the first man-made fibers at the beginning of the twentieth century, synthetics have become ever more sophisticated. Increasingly, fibers are mixed to combine the advantages of their different qualities. For example, more and more ready-to-wear garments made using mainly natural fiber fabrics also include a small percentage of spandex (Lycra) as it helps the garment to keep its shape. As a sewer, it is useful to understand each fiber's particular qualities so you can properly assess the fabric you are buying.

COTTON

The most widely used natural fiber, cotton is highly versatile, so it can be woven into endless different weights and qualities and dyed in myriad shades. It is also very resilient, and so can be given special finishes to improve the body and wear. Easy to launder and cool on the skin, it is a favorite breathable fabric for summer and makes for excellent winter layering under warmer outer layers.

Sewing user friendliness: very

WOOL

Sheep provide most of our wool, but it can also be spun from goats' coats (cashmere and mohair), rabbit (angora), or llama (alpaca, vicuna). Unlike fur or hair, wool has a naturally crimped quality that makes it easy to weave into many different weights and qualities, from fine challis, which is made to use for dresses, to elegant worsteds for suits and coarser tweeds. Wool does not crease easily and is valued by tailors because it can be steamed, sculpted, and encouraged into shape. It dyes well into beautiful subtle colors. Designed to protect animals in cold climates, wool naturally keeps you warm in winter. However, it is a high-maintenance fabric, holds water, shrinks readily, and pills easily, so is best dry cleaned. For sewers, it is not slippery, but can fray easily.

Sewing user friendliness: easy

LINEN

Spun from the long, waxy fibers of the flax plant, linen has a natural luster and three times the strength of cotton. It doesn't take dye as well as cotton, which results in richer, plain colors where the pattern is generally woven into rather than printed onto the fabric. Because it creases readily, people either love or avoid linen. On the plus side, linen presses beautifully, looks sophisticated, and linings and interfacings can help reduce creasing in the finished garment. Very cool on the skin, it is an excellent summer fabric.

Sewing user friendliness: very

Cotton variations

Here's a sample of different kinds of cotton weaves that can also be used in combination with other fibers. From top left, clockwise: Small-scale printed pin dots are a patchwork favorite; crinkled white stripes teamed with flat green-blue are classic small-scale seersucker; cotton jersey is a knitted fabric that offers a soft stretch drape; printed cotton comes in endless colors and designs; woven stripes look the same on both sides of the fabric and naturally follow the straight of grain; gingham is a popular tightly woven cotton, best known for its checked designs in various sizes.

SILK

This fine, lustrous fiber is spun by silkworms as they make their cocoons. Silk is an excellent insulator that evolved to keep the pupae at an even temperature whatever the outside conditions. In turn, it will keep you cool in summer while providing surprising warmth when needed. Originating in China, silk can be woven into richly colored fabrics from fine chiffons to rich exotic brocades. Silk is a soft, fluid fabric that skims the contours for lingerie and feels wonderful against the skin, but its naturally slippery quality makes it something of a challenge to sew.

Sewing user friendliness: tricky

Synthetic fibers

Man-made fabrics are becoming increasingly sophisticated and it's no longer true, for example, that natural fibers have the monopoly on breathability. With a view to improving fabrics for sportswear, the textiles industry has invested heavily in wickable fabrics that draw moisture away from the skin. Sportswear has also been the inspiration behind super-stretch fibers such as spandex (Lycra). This can be used as a pure 100 percent fabric, or incorporated into fabrics that are made up mainly of natural fibers but could do with a little extra elasticity to pull them back into shape. Each synthetic has different qualities and the main ones are outlined in more detail in the Fabric Dictionary (pages 236–237). However, synthetics are generally shinier, more slippery, and easier to care for than their natural cousins. Many also have a lot more stretch. For these reasons, they can be more difficult to handle than natural fabrics.

Sewing user friendliness: moderate

Judge the drape

Although you might expect a fine, loose woven silk like this to have little or no body, this is not always the case. Depending on how it has been treated and woven, even the finest fabric could have plenty of drape. Hold the material up on the diagonal, and if the folds fall full and wide like this, you can be sure it will have plenty of body, and even if you plan to use it only as a "flat" panel, it will have more life and will look crisper at the window (see opposite page).

TRIMMINGS AND FASTENINGS

The secret to successful use of trimmings is to add them in a similar way to seasoning a recipe. Used sparingly, they add interest, intensify the ingredients and bring personality to the dish. As the trimmings are an essential part of the design, you need to choose and buy them at the same time as the main fabric. Here are some of the main types.

Piping, cording, and bias binding

These are all variations on a theme based on bias binding. Discretion is their strength: they all offer a neat edging that can completely change the personality of the project, depending on the color you choose. Pipe or bind anything to match the main fabric for elegant restrained style, or choose a vibrant contrast for a more extrovert look. Because piping, cording and bias binding are neat and discreet, they'll never overwhelm the piece, so you can afford to be brave with the color if you so wish.

Bias binding is made from strips of fabric cut across the grain at 45 degrees to the straight edge. You can buy bias binding in a selection of widths and many colors, or you can make your own, and then use it to bind edges (pages 230–231). Piping is bias binding that is stitched into, rather than over, the seam. Cording is piping with a filler cord running through it (confusingly, most of us know this as piping). You can buy ready-made cording in a range of sizes from fabric stores and notions departments.

Ribbons and bows

Ribbons range from glossy double satin and sheer organza to exotic woven jacquard, chunky grosgrain, and luxurious velvet in widths of ⅛" (3 mm) to a bold 3" (7.5 cm). They're generally designed to be surface stitched onto the piece, although wider ribbons can be stitched between seams for a piping effect. Use them in contrast to the main fabric to make a statement or more discreetly to add quality (down the inside of a button band of a cardigan, for example, so it is glimpsed when the garment is open).

Braids, fringes, and tapes

Richly woven braids with their textured edges, are generally surface mounted on furnishings or heavier garments, such as jackets and coats. Fringes of all kinds—fabric, beaded, feathered—are usually mounted on braid, which is used as a base for stitching the fringe into the seam.

Twill and other woven tapes have their roots in utility pajama tape. Often made in cotton, they are now available in a wide range of widths, colors, and designs with a natural, unpretentious appeal.

Ribbon ranges

Ribbon trimmings can totally change the personality of a garment. These represent some of the main types, from bottom left: narrow green velvet is a pretty, feminine choice for eveningwear; red gingham, available in many widths and bright colors, lends a fun, country feel; the sheer cream organza adds pretty, feminine appeal; striped grosgrain was the ribbon of choice for Edwardian boaters (straw hats), and is still very popular today for both men's and women's garments; pure silk picot edged ribbon would add quality to any garment, especially in this restrained mossy green shade.

Keeping it together

You can either keep your fastenings secret, hidden from view so as not to spoil the line of the garment, or you can promote them, letting them multi-task as trimmings. This is not a new thing: buttons have always had trimming potential—not only in their intrinsic style, but also in how you use them. You might make a statement by fastening a coat using two huge buttons, or you may design a long row of tiny pearl buttons all the way down the back of a wedding dress. Both have a dramatic effect on the garment. Revealed zippers can also be used as part of a design, immediately transforming what might have been a classic item to one with utility edginess. With the recent fashion for underwear as outerwear, rows of revealed hooks and eyes allude to corsetry, while snaps, especially larger ones, imply camping and outdoor life.

Buttons

There's something irresistible about buttons. They can be made from almost any material and be big, small, simple, or intricate and have the power to completely change the look of a garment. When buying them, try

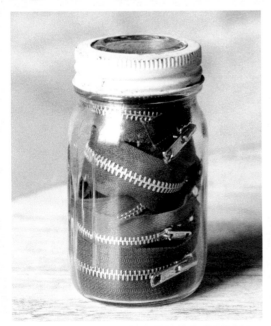

to visualize the space the buttons will occupy to make sure there's an overall balance. For example, two large buttons might make a statement, but six might use the space better, providing a better balance.

Zippers

One of the most useful fastenings available, there are several different kinds of zippers, suitable for different situations ranging from tiny nylon ones for children's clothes to huge outdoor types suitable for luggage, camping equipment, and marquees.

METAL zippers are the originals, consisting of two lines of interlocking teeth set within a tape. They're generally bulkier and showier than their nylon equivalents.
NYLON zippers come in myriad colors with perfectly matched tapes and teeth; they are the most popular type.
INVISIBLE zippers have a pair of coils instead of two rows of teeth. These sit neatly behind the tapes when closed so the zipper just looks like part of the seam.
OPEN-ENDED zippers are for garments, such as jackets.
CONTINUOUS zippers made from nylon are also sold by the yard (meter) with one slider per yard (meter). They're used where long lengths are required, such as for upholstery and window-seat cushion covers. Simply snip off the length needed.

Hooks, snaps, and secret fastenings

HOOKS AND EYES for their size, have extraordinary strength. Skirt and trouser hooks, for example, need to take the strain of a close fit and constant movement.
SNAPS that are sewn on are traditional, but you can also buy a wide range of the no-sew snaps, studs, rivets, and jeans buttons. These are fixed in position using pliers or a special tool, which usually comes as part of the kit.
ELASTIC might not be a fastening but it does enable getting in and out of garments. Available from thread-like shirring elastic, which can be used with a sewing machine, up to 3" (7.5 cm) wide.
HOOK-AND-LOOP TAPE provides strong, discreet fastenings. It is available in strips, which can be cut to length, or as dots.

THE
PROJECTS

MAKING THE PROJECTS

The collection of projects in this section has been designed to provide you with the core skills needed to make almost anything you might want to sew. With the exception of two garments—the Summer Dress and the Hacking Jacket—each of the projects has been designed with the beginner sewer in mind. There are projects to make for the home, wardrobe staples, and one-off pieces. The step-by-step instructions have been written and illustrated so that, depending on your skill level, they can be read in different ways—either at-a-glance or more in-depth.

Using the patterns

PRINT The patterns on the enclosed CD-rom are in PDF format. For the best results, open the files using Adobe Acrobat Reader. (For the latest free version, please visit http://www.adobe.com.com.) You may also bring PDF images into a number of other image programs and design programs, but some default software on computers may not give the best results. Once you have opened the desired pattern file, check your printer settings; it should be set to print at "actual size" —not "fit to page" —to ensure that the pattern sizes will be accurate. Print the pages on 8½" x 11" (22cm x 28cm) printer paper. After printing, measure the 1" x 1" (2.54cm x 2.54cm) square on each page to make sure your pattern printed at the correct size.

When assembling the patterns, match the letters along the edge of each page with the same letter on the adjoining page. Overlap each page slightly so that the pages align at the letter/number markers. Tape the pages together, and then cut out the pattern pieces using paper scissors.

PHOTOCOPY Take the book to a photocopy shop where you can have the individual pattern pages copied, enlarging them by the percentage given to provide full-size patterns.

ENLARGE ONTO GRAPH PAPER For this you'll need dressmaker's graph paper, which is marked with ⅜" (1 cm) and 2" (5 cm) squares. Each small graph square on the gridded patterns in the book represents a ⅜" (1 cm) square on the dressmaker's paper so the lines can be transferred.

Skill levels and project difficulty ratings

The different sections of the book have been designed to work together to make the projects easy to follow for an absolute beginner and sewing enthusiasts alike.

✎ ABSOLUTE BEGINNERS are best advised to start with a project with a one-button difficulty rating. The projects are accompanied with fully illustrated step-by-step instructions, but beginners who are not familiar with key sewing terms can refer to the detailed explanations of the various techniques in the Basic Sewing Skills section. Start with one-button projects.

✎ SEWERS WITH BASIC SEWING SKILLS who are familiar with general sewing terms should be able to follow the full project instructions in conjunction with the illustrations. Look out for one-, two-, three-, and four-button projects.

✎ SEASONED STITCHERS who are experienced and adept at sewing may not need to read the full project instructions, but be able to follow the at-a-glance step headings and illustrations. Choose from any of the projects, regardless of its button rating.

Choosing the right size

All the garments in the book are given in US women's sizes 6 to 14, with the exception of the pajama pants, which come in four unisex sizes, the vest, which comes in men's sizes, and the girl's dress.

Difficulty ratings

Each project has been given a difficulty rating indicated by button icons.

⚫⚫ ⚫⚫ ⚫⚫ ⚫⚫ ⚫⚫—straight and curved seams only: best choice for beginners

⚫⚫ ⚫⚫ ⚫⚫ ⚫⚫ ⚫⚫—both straight and curved seams, inserting zippers

⚫⚫ ⚫⚫ ⚫⚫ ⚫⚫ ⚫⚫—straight and curved seams, inserting zippers, easing fabric

⚫⚫ ⚫⚫ ⚫⚫ ⚫⚫ ⚫⚫—all of the above, but with more individual pattern pieces

⚫⚫ ⚫⚫ ⚫⚫ ⚫⚫ ⚫⚫—the trickier projects requiring some basic tailoring such as linings, interfacings, and precision pressing

US sizes	6	8	10	12	14
UK sizes	8	10	12	14	16
EU sizes	34	36	38	40	42
Bust	31½" 80 cm	32½" 83 cm	34" 87 cm	36" 92 cm	38" 97 cm
Waist	24" 61 cm	25" 64 cm	26½" 67 cm	28" 71 cm	30" 76 cm
Hip	33½" 85 cm	34½" 88 cm	36" 92 cm	38" 97 cm	40" 102 cm
Neck to waist	15½" 40 cm	16" 40.5 cm	16¼" 41.5 cm	16½" 42 cm	16¾" 42.5 cm

TUNIC

A classic wardrobe staple, the sleeveless tunic is a versatile item of clothing that can be made from just over a yard and a half (1.4 meters) of fabric. It is easy to make if you decide on a cotton fabric. If you're more experienced, try it in a soft washed silk, like the version shown here.

DIFFICULTY RATING: ⦂⦂ ⦂⦂ ⦂⦂ ⦂⦂ ⦂⦂

The simple tunic has been with us since the Roman tunica, and has never been out of fashion, which is why we chose to include a full-sized pattern of this garment in the book. It's been designed so you can make a flattering long-line top, like the one shown here, a shorter version that would look good with fitted skirts, slacks, or jeans, or, by cutting it longer, a fun young 1960s-style mini dress.

TUNIC SIZES
To fit women's sizes 6, 8, 10, 12, and 14.
The finished lengths of the tunic range from approximately 21" (54 cm) for the short-line top (waist length), 29" (73 cm) for the long-line top (hip length), and 32" (82 cm) for the mini dress (thigh length), but the length is easily adjustable.

FABRIC FINDER
The exquisite coral tones of this washed silk have a vintage-style bloom that lends elegance to the garment. The soft flowing drape skims the bumpy bits while flattering the curves.
Try these alternatives:
Silk crepe de Chine—Laundered fine cotton—Silk-rayon—Cotton jersey—Voile

Materials
1½ yd (1.4 m) of a washed silk, 54" (137 cm) wide, OR 2 yd (1.7 m) of a washed silk, 45" (115 cm) wide
Complementary or contrasting nylon zipper, 20" (50 cm) long
Matching sewing thread

SKILLS SET
Working even slipstitch—**page 208** • Slipstitching double-fold hems—**page 210**
Stitching straight seams—**page 211** • Clipping curved seams—**page 212**
Finishing seams—**pages 214 and 215** • Stitching single-point darts—**page 220**

FRONT-NECK/ARMHOLE FACING
Cut 1 on the fold

BACK-NECK/
ARMHOLE FACING
Cut 2

ENLARGE
BY 500%

Pattern pieces

SIZE 6
SIZE 8
SIZE 10
SIZE 12
SIZE 14

EACH SMALL GRAPH
SQUARE = ⅜" (1 CM)

⅜" (1 CM) ZIPPER
SEAM ALLOWANCE

FRONT
Cut 1 on the fold

BACKS
Cut 2

WAIST LENGTH

WAIST LENGTH

HIP LENGTH

HIP LENGTH

THIGH LENGTH

THIGH LENGTH

Cutting diagram

front-neck/armhole facing

front

front-neck/armhole facing

back

back-neck/
armhole facing

Cutting guide

Press the fabric thoroughly before cutting.

FROM THE FABRIC:

✂ Cut one tunic front and one front-neck/
armhole facing, each on the fold.

✂ Cut two tunic backs and two back-neck/
armhole facings.

A ⅝" (1.5 cm) seam allowance, a ¾" (2 cm)
hem allowance, and ⅜" (1 cm) zipper opening
turnbacks are included on the pattern pieces. (If
you want a slightly longer or shorter skirt, take
this into account when cutting the front and
backs.)

To make the tunic

1 STITCH THE BACK PIECES TOGETHER
With right sides together, pin the tunic back pieces together.
Use the zipper to measure down the back seam and mark the
end stop with a pin. Baste from the pin down to the hem and
stitch, taking a ⅝" (1.5 cm) seam allowance and leaving the zipper
section open. Note that the seam allowance along the zipper
opening is only ⅜" (1 cm). Finish the raw seam edges and press
the seam open.

2 INSERT THE ZIPPER
Insert a revealed zipper so that the zipper
tape is visible on the right side of the back,
folding under the ⅜" (1 cm) seam allowance all
around the zipper.

3 STITCH THE DARTS
Carefully stitch the single-point darts on the tunic front.

Try this...
The method used for sewing the all-in-one neck/armhole facing to the tunic top is a little tricky, but it is especially suitable for silk as all the raw seam edges are hidden inside the facing. If you are using a crisp cotton fabric for the tunic, why not try the easier method of adding the facing used for the Basic Dress on pages 164–169.

4 STITCH THE FRONT TO THE BACK
With right sides together, stitch the side seams and shoulder seams. Finish the seam edges and press the seams open.

5 PREPARE THE FACING
Next, make up the all-in-one neck/armhole facing. With the right sides of the front facing and two back facings together, pin, baste, and stitch the shoulder and side seams. Remove the basting and press the seams open. Press ¼" (6 mm) to the wrong side along the bottom edge of the facing, baste, and stitch.

6 STITCH THE FACING IN PLACE ALONG THE NECK EDGE

Turn the tunic right side out. With right sides together, pin and baste the neck edge of the facing to the raw edge of the tunic neckline. Stitch. Remove the basting. Then trim the seam and clip the curves.

7 STITCH THE FACING IN PLACE ALONG THE ARMHOLE EDGE

Turn the tunic wrong side out and press the facing to the wrong side of the tunic along the neck edge, centering the neck seamline on the fold. Then with right sides together, stitch the facing to the tunic along the armholes, starting and ending the stitching at the shoulder seam. This is a little tricky as you have to pull back the facing in order to stitch the armhole seam. Trim the seams and clip the curves. Press along the folded seam as for the neck edge.

8 SLIPSTITCH THE FACING ALONG THE ZIPPER

At the zipper edges, turn in the raw edges of the facing and slipstitch to the zipper tape.

9 HEM THE TUNIC TOP

For a quick hem, machine stitch it neatly in place. At the hem edge, turn up ⅜" (1 cm) twice, press, and baste. Machine stitch this double hem, stitching close to the first fold.

PAJAMA PANTS

An easy project for a starter sewer. Make these drawstring pajama pants in a fine seersucker, like those shown here, or a warm fleece for cozy nights, and you have a great pair of pajamas suitable both for girls and boys.

DIFFICULTY RATING: ⊞ ⊞ ⊞ ⊞ ⊞

Materials

3 yd (2.5 m) of a striped cotton fabric, 45" (115 cm) wide
2 yd (2 m) of contrasting cotton pajama tape, ⅝" (1.5 cm) wide
Matching sewing thread

Pajama pants are the easiest ever garment to make and to wear. Loose and slouchy, there's no tricky fitting and no fiddly fastenings—when it comes to putting them on, just tighten the tape ties that run around the waistband low on the hips. Learning how to make a drawstring channel for ties is a useful skill for accessories and homewares as well as garments. Although there is one curved seam to sew, it isn't a tightly fitting seam. Basic drawstring pajama pants are a great choice for a first make because you really can't go wrong.

PAJAMA SIZES
Unisex sizes S, M, L, and XL.

FABRIC FINDER
Pajama pants are all about comfort. Natural fibers are best as they absorb moisture, are breatheable, and are pleasant to the touch. Fine seersucker is an excellent summer choice as the crinkles keep the fabric away from the skin for a fabulously cool feel.
Try these alternatives:
Soft fine cotton—Brushed cotton—Cotton flannel—Seersucker—Flannelette—Cotton jersey

SKILLS SET
Slipstitching double-fold hems—page 210
Stitching straight seams—page 211 • Clipping curved seams—page 212
Finishing seams—pages 214 and 215 • Making buttonholes—page 232

FRONTS
Cut 2

WAISTBAND
Cut 1 on fold

BACKS
Cut 2

SIZE S
SIZE M
SIZE L
SIZE XL

EACH SMALL GRAPH
SQUARE = ³⁄₈" (1 CM)

ENLARGE
BY 500%

Pattern pieces

Cutting diagrams

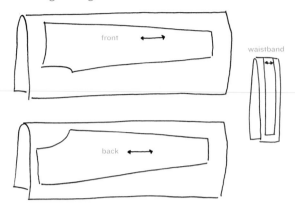

front

waistband

back

Cutting guide

Press the fabric carefully before cutting. Precisely cut curves help to make stitching easier.

FROM THE FABRIC:

✄ Cut two front leg pieces and two back leg pieces.

✄ Cut one waistband, on the fold.

A ⅝" (1.5 cm) seam allowance is included on all the pattern pieces, and a 1¼" (3 cm) hem allowance on the bottom edges of the front and back leg pieces.

To make the pajama pants

1 STITCH THE INNER LEG SEAMS
With right sides together, stitch one back leg piece to the corresponding front leg piece along the inside leg seam. Repeat with the other back and front pieces. Finish the raw seam edges and press the seams open.

2 STITCH THE CENTER SEAM
Join the two legs together at the curved center seam. With right sides together, stitch the center seam from waist edge to waist edge. Now re-stitch this seam on top of the first line of stitching to strengthen the seam. Press the seam open, then press to one side. Finish the seam by sewing zigzag stitch through both layers to further strengthen the seam.

3 STITCH THE OUTER SIDE SEAMS
With right sides together, pin the front of the pants to the back. Stitch. Finish the raw seam edges and press the seams open.

4 STITCH ON THE WAISTBAND
Fold the waistband in half widthwise and mark the center point with a pin. Mark two ½" (12 mm) buttonhole positions, one ⅝" (1.5 cm) from each side of the pin and centered on the front section of the waistband—take into account the ⅝" (1.5 cm) seam allowance on the waistband. Machine stitch the buttonholes. With right sides together, the raw edges aligned, and the center pin aligned with the center front seam, pin the waistband to the pajamas. Where the ends of the waistband meet at the center back, fold them under to align with the seamline and press. Place these ends right sides together and stitch along the fold. Trim and press the seam open. Pin the waistband back in position, baste in place, and stitch ⅝" (1.5 cm) from the edge. Press the seam and waistband upward.

5 FINISH THE WAISTBAND
Press under ⅝" (1.5 cm) along the free raw edge of the waistband. Pin this edge to the back of the waistband so it covers the line of stitching just completed. Baste then topstitch the waistband in place along the waistband seam.

6 HEM THE PANTS AND ADD THE DRAWSTRING
Turn up ⅝" (1.5 cm) twice around the bottom edges of the pant legs to form a double hem. Press and baste. Stitch the hem close to the first fold. Lastly, thread the waistband tape through the waistband and hem the ends.

Try this...
The top of the stitching as you sew is always the better quality stitch. On areas where topstitching is used always work on the side of the garment that is going to show.

BUTTON-BACK BLOUSE

You'll want to make this button-back blouse over and over again. It's fun, flattering, and easy to sew, Create a completely different look by making the blouse in a glowing shade of plain silk for an elegant evening top or try making it in soft cotton lawn for warm summer days.

DIFFICULTY RATING:

This blouse flatters any figure. It is also easy to make because the yoke is the only fitted part, so there's no pattern adjustment to worry about. However, the blouse has been given a three-button difficulty level because there are set-in sleeves. Nonetheless, it is an excellent project for a first-time sleeve setter because its relaxed design is more forgiving than a tailored piece.

If you are a total beginner, you may also be worried about making the buttonholes. This shouldn't be too challenging if your machine has a buttonhole setting, but do try them out on spare fabric first. If you're not fully confident, sew on large snaps instead and place buttons on top for the same effect.

BLOUSE SIZES
To fit women's sizes 6, 8, 10, 12, and 14.

FABRIC FINDER
The fullness of the bodice means that a softly draping lightweight fabric would be the most flattering choice.
Try these alternatives:
Silk or polyester crepe de Chine—Habotai—Charmeuse—
Soft cotton lawn—Chambray

Materials
1¾ yd (1.6 m) of a polka-dot print, 45″ (115 cm) wide
Matching sewing thread
20″ (50 cm) of contrasting narrow ready-made piping, for yoke decoration
16″ x 20″ (40 cm x 50 cm) of lightweight iron-on interfacing
Five button molds, for ¾″ (2 cm) covered buttons, or five ¾″ (2 cm) buttons
Scrap of contrasting fabric (matching piping), to cover buttons (extra if making your own piping)

SKILLS SET
Stitching straight seams—page 211 • Clipping curved seams—page 212 • Stitching French seams—page 216
Sewing single-point darts—page 220 • Hand gathering—page 222 • Easing—page 223
Making buttonholes—page 232 • Adding buttons—page 233

ENLARGE BY 500%

Pattern pieces

SIZE 6
SIZE 8
SIZE 10
SIZE 12
SIZE 14

EACH SMALL GRAPH SQUARE = ⅜" (1 CM)

SLEEVE
Cut 2

BACK-NECK FACING
Cut 2

FRONT YOKE
Cut 1 on fold

FRONT
Cut 1 on fold

BACK
Cut 2

FOLDLINE

FOLDLINE

FOLDLINE

CUFF
Cut 2

FRONT-NECK FACING
Cut 1 on fold

Cutting diagram

front yoke   front-neck facing

front

back-neck facing

sleeve

back

cuff

Cutting guide

Launder and press the fabric thoroughly
before cutting.

FROM THE FABRIC:

� Cut one blouse front, one front yoke, and
one front-neck facing, all on the fold.

� Cut two blouse backs, two back-neck facings,
two sleeves, and two cuffs.

FROM THE IRON-ON INTERFACING:

� Cut one front-neck facing on the fold and
two back-neck facings.

A ⅝" (1.5 cm) seam allowance is included on all the
pattern pieces, and a ¾" (2 cm) hem allowance on the
bottom edges of the blouse front and backs.

To make the blouse

1 **PREPARE THE FRONT**

Stitch the two darts on the front and press them downward.
Pin and baste the ready-made piping to the right side of the top
of the front, aligning the piping seamline (as close to the piping
as possible) with the front seamline. With right sides together,
pin and baste the front yoke to the front (on top of the piping),
aligning the raw edges of the front and the yoke. Using a zipper
foot, stitch the three layers together. Remove the basting. Press
the seam downward so the piping faces upward. Finish the raw
seam edges together, with zigzag or overlocking stitches.

2 STITCH THE BACKS TO THE FRONT

With the right sides of the backs and the front together, stitch the shoulder and side seams. Press the seams open. Finish all raw edges as the seams are stitched. If you prefer, use the French seam method for the exposed seams (page 216).

3 PREPARE THE NECK FACING

Press the iron-on interfacing onto the wrong sides of the facing pieces. With the right sides together, stitch the front facing to the back facings at the shoulder seams. Press the seams open. Finish the raw edges only along the outside edge of the facing as the shoulder seams will be enclosed under the facing.

4 STITCH ON THE NECK FACING

With right sides together, stitch the facing to the blouse, matching the shoulder seams. The facing does not go all the way to the edge of the back pieces—this is because the center back edges are folded back in the next step to form button and buttonhole bands. Trim the seam and clip the curves. Press the seams open. Turn the facing to the inside and press along the seamline, pressing the exposed seam allowance at the top of the center-back edges downward.

5 STITCH THE BUTTON AND BUTTONHOLE BANDS

Press 1½" (4 cm) to the wrong side all along the center edge of one of the back pieces, pin, and baste. Then press 2" (5 cm) to the wrong side (this will cover the end of the facing at the neck edge). Pin and baste along both sides of the band and along the neck edge. With the wrong side of the blouse facing you, topstitch ⅛" (3 mm) from the band folds, starting at the hem edge on one side of the band and stitching up to the neck edge, along the neck edge and back down to the hemline. Remove the basting and press. Repeat on the other back piece.

6 PREPARE THE SLEEVES

Stitch two lines of gathering stitches across the top of one sleeve, stitching just inside the seam allowance. Do the same across the cuff edge of the sleeve, but stopping and starting the stitching ¾" (2 cm) from the side edges. With right sides together, stitch the sleeve seam, taking care not to catch the ends of the gathering threads in the seam. Mark the center of the top of the sleeve with a pin. Repeat on the other sleeve.

7 STITCH THE SLEEVES TO THE BLOUSE

Turn the blouse wrong side out and one sleeve right side out. Slip the sleeve into the armhole with raw edges aligned. Match the shoulder seam with the sleeve top center point marked with the pin and align the sleeve seam with the blouse side seam. Pin then baste the lower part of the sleeve in position between the ends of the gathering threads. Pull up the gathering threads so that the sleeve top fits the armhole. Adjust the gathers so they are even and pin, then baste in position. Stitch. Next, work a second line of stitching ¼" (6 mm) from the first line. Trim the seam to just outside the second line of stitching and finish the raw edges. Turn the blouse right side out and press the seam toward the sleeve. Repeat with the other sleeve.

8 STITCH ON THE CUFFS

With right sides together, stitch the short edges of one of the cuffs together to form a ring. Press the seam open. Pull up the gathering threads at the bottom of one of the sleeves until it matches the circumference of the cuff. With right sides together, pin the cuff to the gathered sleeve, adjusting the gathers so they are even and fit the cuff. Baste and stitch. Press ⅝" (1.5 cm) to the wrong side along the raw edge of the cuff, then fold this edge to the inside of the sleeve, making sure the inside of the cuff overlaps the stitching line. Slipstitch in place. Repeat with the other cuff.

9 HEM THE BLOUSE

Press ⅜" (1 cm) to the wrong side twice along the hemline edge of the blouse to form a double hem. Pin and baste. Stitch close to the first fold.

10 MAKE THE BUTTONS AND BUTTONHOLES

Cover the button molds if you are making fabric-covered buttons. Mark the positions of the vertical buttonholes in the center of the right back band—the top of the first buttonhole should be ¼" (6 mm) below the neck edge and the bottom of last buttonhole 6" (15 cm) above the hemline. Machine stitch the buttonholes and sew on the buttons.

 Try this...

If you're using really floppy fabric, you may want to add iron-on interfacing to the button and buttonhole bands. Cut two strips of interfacing 1½" (4 cm) wide and as long as the center back edge. After pressing the folds for the back bands and before stitching the bands, open out and press on the interfacing between the folds.

FLOOR CUSHION

Box cushions are surprisingly easy to make, especially if you topstitch the edges for a smart finish. Once you've mastered the art of making them, you'll be able to re-cover sofa and chair cushions, or make generous garden or window seat cushions.

DIFFICULTY RATING:

Materials

1¾ yd (1.6 m) of a medium-weight to heavyweight furnishing fabric print, at least 45" (115 cm) wide, for main fabric

¾ yd (60 cm) of the same weight furnishing fabric in a contrasting print, for sides

Nylon zipper to match main fabric, 27¾" (70 cm) long

Matching sewing thread

Box cushion to fit finished cover

A generously proportioned box cushion works well on the floor and is so much more tailored than a beanbag or pouffe. Made in a neutral tone, it will team with almost any interior scheme. Made supersize like this for the floor, you can use them to provide extra coffee-table height seating when all other chairs are occupied, or even allocate one as a smart living-room dog bed.

CUSHION SIZE
The finished floor cushion measures 27¾" x 27¾" x 4" (70 cm x 70 cm x 10 cm).

FABRIC FINDER
Floor cushions take a lot of wear and tear and should be covered in a furnishing fabric suitable for upholstery, which will be durable and meet all the necessary fire regulations. Machine-washable fabric is best—check the care label and wash to pre-shrink before stitching.
Try these alternatives:
Heavy-duty pure linen—Heavy-duty pure cotton—Linen union—Cotton duck—Canvas—Ticking

SKILLS SET
Stitching straight seams—page 211 • Finishing seams—pages 214 and 215
Inserting a centered zipper—pages 224 and 225 • Topstitching edges to imitate piping—step 5 on page 55

Cutting guide

Press the fabric thoroughly before cutting. Measure and mark the fabric, using a steel ruler, and ensure all the corners are at perfect right angles before cutting.

FROM THE MAIN FABRIC:

✄ Cut one piece for the top, measuring 29" x 29" (73 cm x 73 cm).

✄ Cut two pieces for the bottom, one measuring 29" x 22¾" (73 cm x 58 cm) and the other 29" x 7¼" (73 cm x 18 cm).

FROM THE CONTRASTING FABRIC:

✄ Cut four pieces for the sides, each measuring 29" x 5¼" (73 cm x 13 cm).

To make the floor cushion

1 INSERT THE ZIPPER
As linen frays readily, finish all the edges first. Next, fold under and press a ⅝" (1.5 cm) seam allowance along one long edge of each bottom piece. Open out the folds and with right sides together baste along the fold—this is the seam the zipper goes in. Stitch together ⅝" (1.5 cm) at each end of the seam, leaving the center 27¾" (70 cm) open for the zipper. Lay the joined bottom face down and place the closed zipper face down on top, centered on the seam. Baste and stitch the centered zipper in place. Remove all the basting, then press the zipper opening from the front.

2 STITCH THE SIDES TO THE TOP
With right sides together, pin a contrasting side piece to one edge of the top piece. Starting ⅝" (1.5 cm) in from one corner, stitch the seam leaving a ⅝" (1.5 cm) seam allowance and stopping ⅝" (1.5 cm) before you reach the end of the seam. Sew on the remaining three sides in the same way. Press the seams open.

3 STITCH THE SIDES TO THE BOTTOM

Stitch the bottom of the cushion cover to the sides, stitching each seam in the same direction and sequence as you did for the top. Press the seams open.

4 STITCH THE CORNERS

Stitch the corner seams, stopping at the seamline for nice crisp corners. Press these short corner seams open. Next, press all the long seams flat toward the contrasting sides.

Try this...

When adding the bottom, always stitch following the same sequence and in the same direction as for the front. This is so that the cushion cover will lie square. If you stitch in the opposite direction, you may get a cross pull.

5 TOPSTITCH THE EDGES

Unzip and turn the cover right side out. Then fold exactly along each seamline to sandwich the seam allowance between the layers, and press. This will make the topstitching easier. Topstitch along all the seams 1/8" (3 mm) from the edge for an instant faux piping effect. Insert the cushion and close the zipper.

EDGE-TO-EDGE JACKET

Cut short and simple, this jacket is more casual than a work jacket but smarter than a cardigan. Make it in either wool or linen and wear it over dresses, skirts, or jeans.

DIFFICULTY RATING:

Many classic jackets are frankly difficult to make, especially when they involve linings, tricky collars, set-in sleeves, and pockets—this is where dressmaking borders on tailoring. But here's a jacket that is easy to sew. It's collarless, edge-to-edge, and lining-free, so dodges all the difficult tasks while offering the basic elements of jacket construction.

JACKET SIZES
To fit women's sizes 6, 8, 10, 12, and 14.

FABRIC FINDER
Lightweight wool is an excellent mid-season choice that would get you through spring and fall. It also resists creasing and drapes well for a stay-smart look.
Try these alternatives:
Bouclé wool weave—Wool tweed—Wool twill—Wool blends—
Linen and linen blends

Materials
2 yd (1.8 m) of wool fabric, 54" (137 cm) wide
32" x 20" (80 cm x 50 cm) of lightweight iron-on interfacing
1¾ yd (1.5 m) of satin ribbon, ⅜" (1 cm) wide
Six buttons, 1" (2.5 cm) in diameter
Sewing thread to match main fabric
Sewing thread to match ribbon

SKILLS SET
Working even slipstitch—**page 208**
Stitching straight seams—**page 211** • Clipping curved seams—**page 212**
Finishing seams—**pages 214 and 215** • Easing—**page 223**

FRONTS
Cut 2

BACK
Cut 1 on the fold

FRONT FACINGS
Cut 2

BACK-NECK FACING
Cut 1 on the fold

SLEEVES
Cut 2

Pattern pieces

SIZE 6
SIZE 8
SIZE 10
SIZE 12
SIZE 14

EACH SMALL
GRAPH SQUARE =
³⁄₈" (1 CM)

ENLARGE
BY 500%

Cutting diagram

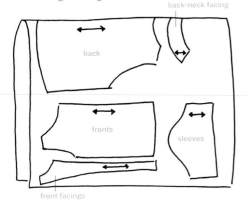

back-neck facing

back

fronts

sleeves

front facings

Cutting guide

Press the fabric thoroughly before cutting.

FROM THE FABRIC:

✄ Cut two jacket fronts, two front facings and two sleeves.

✄ Cut one jacket back and one back-neck facing, both on the fold.

A ⅝" (1.5 cm) seam allowance is included on all the pattern pieces, and a 2¼" (5.5 cm) hem allowance on the bottom edges of the fronts, back, and sleeves. Note that the front facings are shorter than the jacket front pieces.

To make the jacket

1 STITCH THE BACK AND FRONTS TOGETHER
Machine stitch a line of staystitching around the neckline on both fronts and the back. With right sides together, stitch the shoulder seams and the side seams. Finish the raw seam edges and press the seams open. Turn up and stitch a ⅜" (1 cm) hem all along the bottom edge of the jacket.

2 PREPARE THE FACING
Cut out and press the iron-on interfacing onto the wrong sides of the front facings and back-neck facing. With right sides together, stitch the shoulder seams of the prepared facing pieces. Press the seams open. Turn in and stitch a ⅜" (1 cm) hem to the wrong side along the inside edge of the prepared facing.

3 STITCH ON THE FACING
Pin the facing to the jacket with right sides together, matching the shoulder seams, then the back neckline between these, each front edge, and finally pin along each short end of the facing. Baste and stitch. Trim the seams and cut off the jacket hems below the facing to align with the bottom of the facing as shown, but be sure to leave an overlap on the jacket hem that will be hidden behind the facing. Snip off the corners of the seam allowances at the hem edge. Clip the curved seams around the neckline.

4 **BASTE THE HEM IN PLACE**
Turn the facing to the inside of the jacket, turning up the hemline by 1¾" (4.5 cm) to lie behind the end of the facing. Pin and baste the entire hem in position.

5 **ADD THE RIBBON TRIM**
Starting at the facing on the inside of the jacket (see step 4) and over to the front of the jacket, pin and baste the ribbon in position at the top of the hemline about 1" (2.5 cm) from the hemline fold, and continue the ribbon all along the hem and over onto the other facing. Topstitch the ribbon in place, stitching close to each edge. On the inside of the jacket, slipstitch the end of the facing to the jacket hem.

6 **PREPARE THE SLEEVES**
At the top of the sleeves, work two lines of easing stitches. With right sides together, stitch the sleeve seams. Finish the raw seam edges and press the seams open. Turn up ⅜" (1 cm) around the bottom edges of the sleeves and stitch.

7 **STITCH ON THE SLEEVES**
Turn the sleeves right side out and the jacket wrong side out. Pin the right sides of one sleeve and one armhole together, matching the dots. Baste from the side seam up to the lower dot on one side. Return to the side seam and baste up to the other dot. Pull up the easing threads until the sleeve fits the armhole. Distribute the gathers evenly and baste the sleeve in position. Stitch. Repeat with the other sleeve. Clip the underarm curved seams.

8 **FINISH THE SLEEVE HEMS**
Turn up the sleeve hem as for the jacket fronts and back and baste it in place. Now add the ribbon trim. Measure 1" (2.5 cm) from the hem fold at several points around the sleeve and pin the ribbon in position. Baste, then topstitch close to each edge.

9 **STITCH ON THE BUTTONS**
Stitch three buttons to each front, 1¼" (3 cm) from the front edge—position the top button about 4¼" (11 cm) below the neck edge and the other two 1¾" (4.5 cm) apart below the first.

PENCIL SKIRT

Easy to sew, skirts are an excellent first garment project. Admittedly, some sewers find zippers a little difficult to insert so take your time and baste at every stage. A pencil skirt like this one is a useful classic pattern.

DIFFICULTY RATING: ⊞ ⊞ ⊞ ⊞ ⊞

Materials

1 yd (90 cm) of a cotton print, 54" (137 cm) wide, OR 1½ yd (1.3 m) of a cotton print, 45" (115 cm) wide

Matching invisible zipper, 7" (18 cm) long

Two small hooks and eyes

Matching sewing thread

Learn to make this basic skirt, and you'll have all the skills to make almost any skirt you want. The key elements are stitching darts, inserting zippers, and sewing on waistbands. Use exactly the same methods to make easy-to-wear A-lines, a shorter mini, or even something long.

PENCIL SKIRT SIZES
To fit women's sizes 6, 8, 10, 12, and 14.

FABRIC FINDER
A pencil skirt can be made from any fabric you like. But if you are making one for the first time, choose a fabric that will be easy to stitch—a cotton fabric that is neither too thick nor too thin. If it is for the office, stick to sophisticated prints in dark tones. The herringbone weave of this mixed-fiber fabric is smart enough to take you anywhere, while giving the skirt a flattering drape.
Try these alternatives:
Laundered cotton—Denim—Challis—Lightweight wool and wool blends—Jacquard—Linen and linen blends—Gabardine—Lightweight twill

SKILLS SET
Working even slipstitch—**page 208** • Slipstitching double-fold hems—**page 210**
Stitching straight seams—**page 211** • Finishing seams—**pages 214 and 215**
Stitching single-point darts—**page 220** • Inserting an invisible zipper—**pages 228 and 229**

ENLARGE BY 500%

Pattern pieces

6-8
10
12-14

6-8
10
12-14

6-8
10
12-14

6-8
10
12-14

FRONT
Cut 1 on the fold

BACK
Cut 1 on the fold

WAISTBAND
Cut 1

—— SIZE 6
—— SIZE 8
—— SIZE 10
—— SIZE 12
—— SIZE 14

EACH SMALL GRAPH SQUARE = $\frac{3}{8}$" (1 CM)

Cutting diagram

Cutting guide

Press the fabric thoroughly before cutting.

FROM THE FABRIC:
✂ Cut one skirt front and one skirt back, both on the fold.
✂ Cut one waistband.

A ⅝" (1.5 cm) seam allowance is included on all the pattern pieces, and a 1" (2.5 cm) hem allowance on the bottom edges of the skirt front and back.

To make the pencil skirt

1 STITCH THE DARTS
Stitch the four darts on the skirt front and the two darts on the skirt back. Press the darts toward the center.

2 STITCH THE SIDE SEAMS AND INSERT THE ZIPPER
With right sides together, pin the skirt front to the skirt back along the side seams. Using a ⅝" (1.5 cm) seam allowance, insert the invisible zipper in the left side-seam of the skirt, and complete the seam from the bottom of the zipper to the hem. (When the wrong side of the front of the skirt is facing you, the zipper opening is on the left of the front piece.) Next, stitch the right side seam all the way from the waist edge to the hem edge. Press the seams open and finish the raw seam edges.

3 STITCH THE WAISTBAND TO THE SKIRT
Turn the skirt right side out. Fold the waistband in half lengthwise and mark the center point with a pin. With right sides together, pin the waistband to the skirt. Start by matching the marker pin with the right side seam then work around the waistband until you reach the zipper. Stitch ⅝" (1.5 cm) from the raw edges. Trim the seam.

4 PRESS THE WAISTBAND SEAM
Press open the waistband seam, then press the waistband and all the fabric within the seams upward.

5 COMPLETE THE WAISTBAND
Press under ⅝" (1.5 cm) along the free raw edge of the waistband. Pin this edge to the back of the waistband so it covers the line of stitching just completed. Tuck the raw short edges to the inside of the waistband so they enclose the ends of the zipper tape. Baste then topstitch the waistband in place along the waistband seam. Slipstitch the short edges of the waistband together to finish. Press the completed waistband. Stitch the hooks onto one end of the waistband and the eyes to the other.

6 HEM THE SKIRT
For a quick, neat hem, machine stitch it neatly in place. To do this, turn up ½" (12 mm) twice along the hem, press, and baste. Machine stitch this double hem, stitching close to the first fold.

Try this...

To give your waistband some added stiffness, press iron-on interfacing onto the front half of the band. And when topstitching the finished waistband, topstitch both the top and bottom edges.

SUMMER DRESS

This empire-line dress flatters every figure and its versatility means it can be dressed up with heels or down with sandals. However, as it's made from six main pieces, a midriff band, and pockets, this is a project for more experienced sewers.

DIFFICULTY RATING: ⊞ ⊞ ⊞ ⊞ ⊞

Materials

3 yd (2.8 m) of a medium-weight cotton print, at least 45" (115 cm) wide, for main fabric

1 yd (90 cm) of a lightweight cotton fabric, at least 44" (112 cm) wide, for bodice lining

6" x 24" (15 cm x 60 cm) of lightweight iron-on interfacing, for midriff front

Matching zipper, 14" (35 cm) long

Matching sewing thread

Fabrics are the Unique Selling Point of making-your-own clothes. Unless you have an unlimited budget, off-the-peg clothes are by necessity sold in limited colors to appeal to a wide market. Yet a single dress shape can look very different depending on fabric choice so this is where you can really express your own style. This dress, made from a pattern by Simplicity, is admittedly not the simplest to make with its shaped bodice, pleated skirt, and pockets. But it's well worth the effort. Cut flatteringly to fit only around the neckline and midriff band, the pleated skirt skims obligingly over the hips and falls to an elegant straight hem.

SUMMER DRESS SIZES
To fit women's sizes 6, 8, 10, 12, and 14.

FABRIC FINDER
The structure of this dress demands a fabric with plenty of body for a flattering fit and to emphasize its elegant shape.
Try these alternatives:
Densely woven cotton and cotton blends—Lightweight denim—Chambray—Lightweight wool and wool blends—Jacquard—Shantung—Taffeta

SKILLS SET
Working even slipstitch—**page 208** • Slipstitching double-fold hems—**page 210**
Stitching straight seams—**page 211** • Clipping curved seams—**page 212**
Finishing seams—**pages 214 and 215** • Inserting a lapped zipper—**pages 226 and 227**

ENLARGE BY 500%

Pattern pieces

POCKETS
Cut 2

POCKET FACINGS
Cut 2

BACK BODICES
Cut 2

SKIRT FRONT
Cut 1 on the fold

FRONT BODICE
Cut 1 on the fold, from
main fabric and lining

KNEE LENGTH

BELOW-KNEE LENGTH

SIZE 6
SIZE 8
SIZE 10
SIZE 12
SIZE 14

EACH SMALL GRAPH
SQUARE = ³⁄₈″ (1 CM)

MIDRIFF FRONT
Cut 1 on the fold

SKIRT BACK
Cut 1 on the fold

KNEE LENGTH

BELOW-KNEE LENGTH

Cutting diagrams

MAIN FABRIC

pockets

bodice front

skirt back

skirt front

MAIN FABRIC

bodice back

pocket facings

midriff front

LINING FABRIC

midriff front

bodice back

bodice front

Cutting guide

Press the fabric thoroughly before cutting.

FROM THE MAIN FABRIC AND THE LINING:
✂ Cut two bodice backs.
✂ Cut one bodice front and one midriff front, both on the fold.

FROM THE MAIN FABRIC:
✂ Cut one skirt front and one skirt back, both on the fold.
✂ Cut two pockets and two pocket facings.

FROM THE INTERFACING:
✂ Cut one midriff front.

A ⅝" (1.5 cm) seam allowance is included on all the pattern pieces, and a 1" (2.5 cm) hem allowance on the bottom edges of the skirt front and back. Choose either the longer or shorter length when cutting the skirt pieces.

71

Try this...

You can simplify the design of this dress considerably by omitting the pockets. Adapt the pattern by continuing the line of the front skirt piece to match the shape of the back skirt.

To make the summer dress

1 PREPARE THE BODICE
With right sides together, pine the bodice backs to the bodice front at the shoulder seams. Stitch, taking a ⅝" (1.5 cm) seam allowance throughout. Press the shoulder seams open. Repeat with the front and back bodice lining.

2 STITCH THE BODICE TO THE BODICE LINING
With right sides together, pin the bodice lining to the bodice, matching the shoulder seams and the point of the V-neck. Stitch all along the neck edge and around the armholes. Reinforce the V by re-stitching over the original line of stitching. Trim the seams, clip the curved seams, and clip into the V, all the time being careful not to cut the stitching. Turn the lining to the inside by pulling each back through the front at the shoulder seam. Press.

3 STITCH THE BODICE CENTER BACK SEAM
Open up the whole piece so that you can place the center back edges right sides together. Pin the seam from the bottom of the lining, up, through the seam joining the lining to the bodice at the neck, and then down to the hem of the main bodice piece. Stitch and press the seam open. Turn the lining to the inside and press. Baste the raw edges of the two layers of the bodice front together along the side and bottom edges.

4 PLEAT THE BODICE FRONT
Fold along one solid line at the lower edge of the bodice front and bring the fold to the broken line. Pin. Repeat for the other folds. Baste all along the raw edge through the pleats.

5 STITCH ON THE MIDRIFF FRONT

Start by ironing the interfacing onto the wrong side of the midriff-front piece. With right sides together and raw edges aligned, pin the upper edge of the interfaced midriff front to the lower edge of the bodice front, then pin the midriff-lining to the other side in the same way. Baste through all layers and stitch. Press the midriff front and lining downward, and baste them together along the side and bottom edges.

6 STITCH THE BODICE'S RIGHT SIDE SEAM

With the bodice wrong side out, open out the right side-seam edge of the back bodice and wrap it over the right side-seam edge on the front bodice, with the right sides of the front and back lining together and the right sides of the front and back bodice together and the raw edges aligned. Pin and stitch the right side seam through all four layers.

7 STITCH THE POCKET FACINGS TO THE SKIRT FRONT

With right sides together, pin the pocket facing to the skirt front. Stitch along the curved skirt edge. Trim the seam and clip the curves. Turn the facing to the inside and press. Repeat with the other pocket.

8 STITCH ON THE POCKETS

On the inside of the skirt front, with right sides together and raw edges aligned, pin the pocket piece to the pocket facing. Stitch the curved outer edge, leaving the side seam and top edges unstitched. Repeat with the other pocket.

9 BASTE THE POCKET IN PLACE

Align the top and the side seam raw edges of the pocket and its facing with the skirt front and baste the pockets securely in place along these edges.

10 PREPARE THE SKIRT

With right sides together, stitch the skirt back to the skirt front. On the left seam, stitch from the lower edge to the notch (where the zipper starts), then work a few extra reverse stitches for strength. On the right seam, stitch from the hem to the top. Press the seams open.

11 PLEAT THE SKIRT

Start with one center front pleat by folding along the solid line and folding it to the center front. Pin, placing the pins vertically at the folds. Repeat with the other center front pleat. For the remaining front pleats, fold along the solid lines and bring to the broken lines, pinning as you go. Repeat the whole process on the back of the skirt. Baste across the front and back upper edges of the skirt.

12 STITCH THE SKIRT TO THE BODICE

With right sides together, pin the skirt to the bodice, matching the right side seams and left opening edges. Baste and stitch. Press the seam up toward the bodice and finish the raw seam edges with machine zigzag or overlocking stitches.

13 INSERT THE ZIPPER

Insert the zipper using the lapped method, aligning the top of the teeth with the armhole. Turn the top of the zipper tapes under and slipstitch to neaten.

14 STITCH THE HEM

Machine stitch or slipstitch a double hem along the lower edge of the skirt.

LAUNDRY BAG

Making a channel for a drawstring is the key skill you'll learn when stitching this bag. It's a really useful technique that you'll be able to put to use in so many ways—from bags to garments, such as pajama pants and drawstring skirts.

DIFFICULTY RATING: ⬤ ⬤ ⬤ ⬤ ⬤

Materials

2¼ yd (1.9 m) of a cotton print or check, 45" (115 cm) wide

4" (10 cm) of grosgrain ribbon, 1½" (4 cm) wide

Sewing threads to match fabric and ribbon

Drawstring bags are easy to make and stitching them is a great skill to learn. This one's been made with a gusset to give it a three-dimensional quality for extra room, but you can use the same principles for bags of all sizes and shapes. Adapt the bag to make kids' shoe bags, a ballet bag, or a sport bag, by cutting the main pieces smaller, and simplify by using just a front and back piece, omitting the side panels and base.

LAUNDRY BAG SIZE
The finished bag measures 19" (48 cm) wide x 29" (74 cm) tall x 4¼" (11 cm) deep.

FABRIC FINDER
This embroidered brushed gingham is a great choice for a laundry bag as it's robust yet pretty.
Try these alternatives:
Classic gingham—Cotton duck—Denim—Chambray—Gabardine—Ticking—Brushed cotton—Seersucker

SKILLS SET
Stitching straight seams—**page 211**

Cutting guide

Press the fabric thoroughly before cutting. Determine how you're going to cut the pieces from the fabric, so you leave room to cut the long drawstring strips along the length of the fabric.

FROM THE FABRIC:

✄ Cut one piece for the bag front panel and one for the back panel, each 20" x 37" (50 cm x 93 cm).

✄ Cut two pieces for the side panels, each 5¼" x 37" (13 cm x 93 cm).

✄ Cut one piece for the bag base, measuring 5¼" x 20" (13 cm x 50 cm).

✄ Cut two strips for the drawstrings, each 2" x 69" (5 cm x 175 cm).

✄ Cut one strip for the hanging loop, measuring 2" x 14" (5 cm x 36 cm).

To make the laundry bag

1 MAKE THE DRAWSTRINGS AND THE HANGING LOOP

Fold one of the long drawstring strips in half lengthwise with the wrong sides together and press. Open out the strip, fold ½" (12 mm) toward the center along each long edge, and press. Refold the strip along the center and press again for a ½" (12 mm) drawstring width. Clip each end on the diagonal and topstitch all along the long edge of the drawstring, stitching close to the edge. Repeat for the other drawstring and the hanging loop, but don't cut a diagonal end on the hanging loop.

2 STITCH THE BAG PIECES TOGETHER

With right sides together, pin the long edge of the front panel to the long edge of one side panel. Mark a seam opening from 23½" to 25½" (60 cm to 65 cm) from the bottom edge (this is the position of the drawstring channel). Starting ⅜" (1 cm) from the bottom edge and leaving a ⅜" (1 cm) seam allowance, stitch the panels together all the way to the top edge. Remember to leave 2" (5 cm) open in the seam where marked and make a few extra reverse stitches either side of the opening for strength. Stitch the other side panel to the front in exactly the same way, leaving the opening for the drawstring channel. Stitch the back panel to the side panels in the same way. You now have a rectangular tube. Stitch on the base panel, leaving a ⅜" (1 cm) seam allowance. Press all seams open, and press the seam allowances along the drawstring-channel openings to the wrong side.

3 MAKE THE DRAWSTRING CHANNEL

Turn ⅜" (1 cm) to the wrong side around the top of the laundry bag, press and pin. Topstitch this hem. Next, fold 7" (17 cm) of the top of the bag to the wrong side. Press the fold at the top and baste this turning in place along the fold and along the hem. Stitch all around the bag 4" (10 cm) from the upper folded edge—take the sewing bed off your machine if it detaches. Work another line of stitching 2" (5 cm) below this—make sure these two stitching lines are aligned with the top and bottom of the prepared slit openings for the drawstrings.

4 INSERT THE DRAWSTRING

Starting at the left opening, use a large safety pin to thread one drawstring through the channel on the front, over the outside of the bag at the side panel, then through the channel on the back, so ending up on the other side of the side panel from where you started. Repeat with the other drawstring, this time, starting at the right opening. Knot the ends of the drawstrings.

5 STITCH ON THE HANGING LOOP

Fold the hanging loop in half and pin the ends side by side to the center back, with the raw edges about 3" (7.5 cm) from the top of the bag—approximately 1" (2.5 cm) above the upper stitching line of the drawstring channel. Cut a 3" (8 cm) length of 1½" (4 cm) wide ribbon, fold in the raw edges to form a 1½" (4 cm) square, and pin in place over the ends of the hanging loop. Stitch all around the grosgrain square, close the edge, then stitch an "X" from corner to corner for extra strength.

Try this...

Fabric with strong pattern repeats
need extra care when cutting
out to make sure the—in this
case—hearts are centered on the
front, back, and panels. It's worth
cutting out the pattern pieces in
tracing paper and trying it out,
adjusting the width dimensions if
necessary (don't adjust the length
dimensions otherwise you'll get
in a muddle when positioning the
drawstring channel). If you're a
beginner, choose a fabric with a
less obvious repeat.

BASIC CURTAINS

If you can sew a straight line, then you can make a pair of curtains. They're really not difficult to make, especially if you stitch purpose-made gathering tape at the top for fool-proof perfect pleats.

DIFFICULTY RATING:

The key to sewing perfect curtains is careful measuring at every step to ensure all the angles are square and hemlines straight. You need a large flat surface to work on, and while the professionals might have generously proportioned tables to work on, a clean floor is as good a place as any to lay out the fabric before carefully cutting it to size.

CURTAIN SIZE
The basic curtain can be made to fit any window size.

FABRIC FINDER
These curtains are made in a heavyweight 100 percent cotton, which is easy to handle and always looks smart. Although curtains can be made from almost any fabric, you'll get best results from curtain or upholstery fabrics, which generally cut out the light and come in wider-than-fashion-fabric widths.
Try these alternatives:
Heavyweight linens—Linen union—Curtain-weight silk—Chintz—Jacquard—Duppioni

Materials
Curtain fabric in the
   required amount
Curtain lining fabric in
   the required amount
Curtain heading tape,
   for gathering the
   curtain top
Hooks to fit the curtain
   tape
Matching sewing thread
Two metal curtain-weight
   rings for each curtain

SKILLS SET
Working even and uneven slipstitch—pages 208 and 209
Stitching straight seams—page 211

Measuring guide

FOR THE FINISHED CURTAIN LENGTH:
Measure from the top of the curtain rail to the floor, or to the bottom edge of the windowsill if you want short curtains. The length is know as the curtain "drop."
FOR THE FINISHED CURTAIN WIDTH:
Measure the curtain rail and double this figure. (If you are making a pair of curtains for the rail, then each finished curtain width should be half this amount.)

Cutting guide

FROM THE CURTAIN FABRIC:
Cut a panel of fabric that is as long as the desired curtain "drop" plus 10" (25 cm) extra—this extra amount allows 8" (20 cm) for a double hem at the bottom and a 2" (5 cm) turn-down at the top. The width of the panel should be twice the length of the curtain rail, plus 5¼" (13 cm) extra—this allows for a 2⅝" (6.5 cm) turn-back along each side of the curtain. You might have to stitch together two or more drops to achieve the width you need. If in doubt, show the window dimensions to the sales assistant, who will help you to work out what you need.

FROM THE LINING FABRIC:
Cut a panel of fabric that is 2" (5 cm) shorter than the curtain fabric and 4" (10 cm) narrower.

To make the curtain

1 CUT OUT THE CURTAIN AND LINING PANELS
Determine the size of your finished curtain as explained in the Measuring Guide, then cut out the curtain and lining panels as explained in the Cutting Guide.

2 HEM THE CURTAIN AND LINING
Press up a 4" (10 cm) hem along the bottom raw edges of the curtain and lining fabrics, then turn up by another 4" (10 cm) and stitch the bottom hem in place on both pieces. Use uneven slipstitch on the curtain fabric and a regular straight machine stitch for the lining hem. Press the hems from the wrong side.

3 STITCH THE LINING TO THE CURTAIN
Now stitch the lining to the curtain along the side edges. With right sides together, position the lining hem 2" (5 cm) higher than the main curtain, measuring several times along its length to ensure it is straight and ensuring the sides are at perfect right angles to the hem. Pin, then machine stitch the side seams together, taking ⅝" (1.5 cm) seam allowances. Press the seams toward the lining and turn right side out.

4 FINISH THE HEM CORNERS
Lay the curtain right side down on a flat surface, making sure the lining is centered on the main fabric—there is 2" (5 cm) more of the curtain fabric at each side edge of the lining. Smooth out any creases. Press. At the hem corners, fold in the raw edge of the curtain fabric at a 45-degree angle to hide it. Slipstitch the diagonal fold in place, using the even slipstitch technique.

5 ADD THE HEADING TAPE

Starting at the hemline, measure the desired length of the curtain (the calculated drop) up to the top. Do this several times across the width of the curtain, marking the length at the top with tailor's chalk, then use a steel ruler to mark the top position along the width of the curtain—it will be about 2" (5 cm) below the raw edges at the top, but this is your chance to slightly adjust the length. Turn both layers to the wrong side along this line and pin, placing the pins at right angles to the curtain top. Place the heading tape along the width of the curtain, close to the top edge and covering the raw edges. Fold in each end of the tape by 1¼" (3 cm), making sure the hook pockets are right side up and the cords are free from where you will be stitching. Pin the gathering tape in position, folding the curtain turn-down under the tape at each end of the tape. Stitch the tape in place along the top edge first; then go back to the first short side and stitch along it, along the lower edge and finally the last short side.

6 COMPLETE THE FINISHING TOUCHES

Lastly, pull up the strings from both ends of the tape, evenly distributing the gathers to your required width, and secure with a knot or use cord tidies (easier for dry cleaning). Put in your curtain hooks and hang the curtain. At the hem, tuck a curtain-weight ring inside the hem at each corner at the bottom of the curtain and stitch it in place.

Try this...

Curtain fabric can be quite thick, so be sure to match your sewing machine needle to the weight of your fabric—a machine needle that is too fine could snap off during stitching.

CIRCULAR SKIRT

Cut as two half circles—or sometimes as one complete circle—circular skirts are simple to make. The inside circle is stitched flat into the waistband, then the folds flow smoothly over the hips, offering fullness at the hem.

DIFFICULTY RATING:

With no darts or gathers to deal with, circular skirts are about the easiest to make. Yet once you've learned the technique, they're surprisingly versatile, taking on a completely different personality depending on the length. Cut it long for floor-sweeping evening elegance, or if you love your legs go thigh high for cheer-leader chirpiness.

SKIRT SIZES
To fit women's sizes 6, 8, 10, 12, and 14.
The finished length is approximately 22½" (58 cm), but the length is easily adjustable.

FABRIC FINDER
Circular skirts can be made from almost any fabric, but aim for one that has body and graceful fluidity. Floor length skirts will need less body as they become very wide at the hem.
Try these alternatives for daywear:
Laundered cotton—Lightweight denim—Chambray—Challis—Seersucker—Silk linen—Cotton jersey
Try these alternatives for eveningwear:
Fine silk—Fine satin—Taffeta—Silk/polyester mixes

Materials
3¼ yd (3 m) of a fine, tightly woven linen print, at least 45" (115 cm) wide
Matching invisible zipper, 9" (23 cm) long
Two buttons, ⅜–½" (1–1.5 cm) in diameter
Matching sewing thread

SKILLS SET
Slipstitching double-fold hems—page 210 • Stitching straight seams—page 211
Finishing seams—pages 214 and 215 • Inserting an invisible zipper—pages 228 and 229
Making buttonholes—page 232 • Adding buttons—page 233

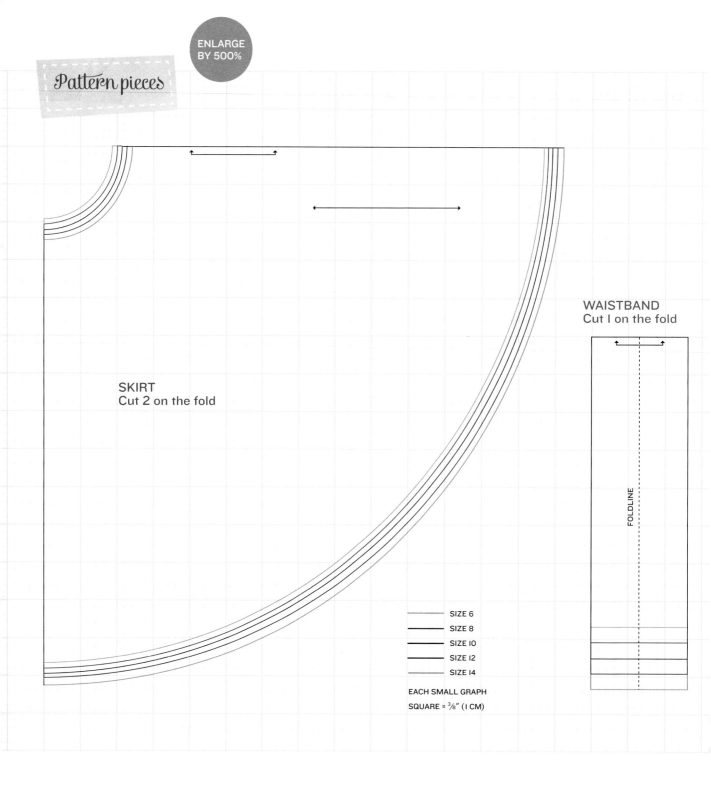

ENLARGE BY 500%

Pattern pieces

SKIRT
Cut 2 on the fold

WAISTBAND
Cut 1 on the fold

FOLDLINE

SIZE 6
SIZE 8
SIZE 10
SIZE 12
SIZE 14

EACH SMALL GRAPH
SQUARE = ⅜" (1 CM)

Cutting diagram

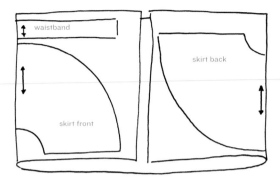

Cutting guide

Press the fabric thoroughly before cutting.

FROM THE MAIN FABRIC:

✂ Cut two skirt pieces, each on the fold—one is for the back and one is for the front.

✂ Cut one piece for the waistband, on the fold.

A ⅝" (1.5 cm) seam allowance is included on all the pattern pieces, and a ⅝" (1.5 cm) hem allowance on the bottom edges of the skirt front and back.

To make the circular skirt

1 STITCH THE SIDE SEAMS AND INSERT THE ZIPPER
With right sides together, pin the front to the back along the side seams. On the left seam, measure down 9⅝" (24.5 cm) from the top edge and mark with a pin. Baste and machine stitch this seam from the pin marker to the hemline. Then insert the invisible zipper into the opening at the top of the seam. Baste and stitch the remaining seam all the way from the top to the bottom. Finish the raw seam edges.

2 PREPARE THE WAISTBAND
With right sides together, fold the waistband piece in half lengthwise and machine stitch along both short ends, ⅝" (1.5 cm) from the edge. Snip off the corners, trim the seams, and press open. Turn the waistband right side out and press the whole waistband in half lengthwise.

3 STITCH ON THE WAISTBAND

With right sides together, pin the waistband to the waistline of the skirt, starting at the back edge of the zipper. Continue pinning the waistband in place until you reach the front edge of the zipper. There will be an extra ⅝" (1.5 cm) of waistband remaining for the buttonhole overlap on the skirt front. Baste and stitch the waistband to the skirt. Press the seam open, and then upward inside the waistband. Firmly press the waistband along the lengthwise fold, then, working on the inside of the skirt, fold in the raw edge, including along the overlap. Pin in position and baste. Slipstitch together the folded edges of the overlap. Then, working from the front side of the skirt, topstitch through all the layers ⅛" (3 mm) from the waist seamline and the same distance from the edge of the overlap.

4 MAKE THE BUTTONHOLES

Mark two buttonholes on the overlap and machine stitch. Sew the buttons into the corresponding positions at the other end of the waistband.

5 HEM THE SKIRT

Because of the shape of a circular skirt, if you tried to stitch a normal 2" (5 cm) deep blind hem, you'd need to accommodate a lot of extra fabric, which would result in unsightly gathers and puckers. For this reason, circular skirts are always finished with a short hem, usually by machine. At the hem edge, press in ¼" (5 mm) to the wrong side all along the bottom edge, then repeat, turning up ⅜" (1 cm) to make a double hem, press, and baste. Machine stitch this double hem close to the first fold.

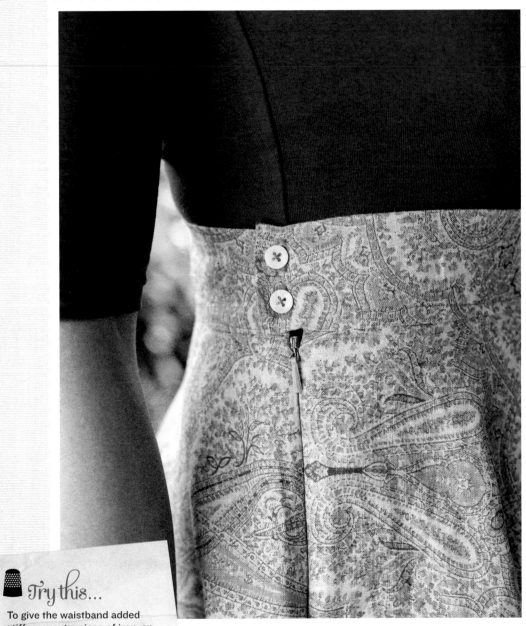

🪡 Try this...

To give the waistband added
stiffness, cut a piece of iron-on
interfacing to the length of the
waistband and half its width,
then press it onto the front half
of the band. When finishing the
waistband, with the right side
facing up, sew around all four
sides, including the upper edge.

TEA DRESS

Ultimately feminine, ultimately flattering, with its soft and wide V neckline, this take-you-anywhere tea dress is surprisingly easy to make.

DIFFICULTY RATING:

Materials

2¼ yd (1.9 m) of a
  synthetic silk fabric,
  54" (137 cm) wide,
  OR 3 yd (2.6 m) of a
  synthetic silk fabric, 45"
  (115 cm) wide
Matching invisible zipper,
  10" (24 cm) long
Matching sewing thread
Four buttons, ¾" (18 mm)
  in diameter

The hallmark pretty prints, flattering cuts that fit yet flow and feminine details like sweetheart necklines, have ensured that the 1940s-style tea dress remains a vintage favorite. What we know as the tea dress is rooted in the late Victorian "tea length dress," which could be anything from knee length to mid calf, designed to take you comfortably from day into early evening. Length isn't such an issue these days, but the principle of a pretty, essentially feminine piece that can be worn plain and simple in the day and dressed up for the evening still holds true. This dress with its flattering wide-cut neckline, softly flowing skirt, and button detail shoulders is an easy-to-make basic.

TEA DRESS SIZES
To fit women's sizes 6, 8, 10, 12, and 14.

FABRIC FINDER
Softly flowing silk works well with the feminine style of the dress, skimming the hips and providing movement in the skirt.
Try these alternatives:
Soft fine cotton—Silk—Silky crepe—Challis—Fine jersey

SKILLS SET
Working even slipstitch—page 208 • Slipstitching double-fold hems—page 210
Stitching straight seams—page 211 • Clipping curved seams—page 212
Finishing seams—pages 214 and 215 • Easing—page 223
Inserting an invisible zipper—pages 228 and 229 • Adding buttons—page 233

SIZE 6
SIZE8
SIZE 10
SIZE 12
SIZE 14

EACH SMALL GRAPH
SQUARE = 3/8" (1 CM)

Pattern pieces

ENLARGE
BY 500%

FRONT
Cut I on the fold

BACK
Cut I on the fold

BACK-NECK FACING
Cut I on the fold

FRONT-NECK FACING
Cut I on the fold

SLEEVE
Cut 2

96

Cutting diagram

front

front-neck facing

back-neck facing

back

sleeves

Cutting guide

Press the fabric carefully before cutting.

FROM THE FABRIC:

✂ Cut one dress front, one dress back, one front-neck facing, and one back-neck facing, each on the fold.

✂ Cut two sleeves.

A ⅝" (1.5 cm) seam allowance is included on all the pattern pieces, and a ¾" (2 cm) hem allowance on the bottom edges of the dress front and back.

To make the tea dress

1 STITCH THE SHOULDER SEAMS
Place the front and back dress pieces with the right sides together and machine stitch the shoulder seams. Then press the seams open. Finish the raw seam edges on seams that will be left exposed as you proceed.

2 PREPARE THE FACING
Stitch together the shoulder seams of the facing pieces, then press them open. Next, make a small hem on the outside edge of the facing. Do this by firmly pressing ⅜" (1 cm) to the wrong side, then machine stitching.

3 STITCH ON THE FACING
Turn the dress right side out and place the facing right side down around the neckline. Align the raw edges and stitch. Cut a V-notch out of the seam at the point of the V-neck. Clip the curves. Press the seams open, then press the facing to the inside of the dress. Secure the facing in position with a couple of small hand stitches at each shoulder seam.

4 PREPARE THE SLEEVES
Press under ⅜" (1 cm) twice along the bottom edge of each sleeve and stitch this double hem in place close to the first fold. At the shoulder edge, run one or two lines of gathering stitches between the markers. Mark the center of the sleeve top with a pin.

5 STITCH ON THE SLEEVES
Turn the dress inside out. Now pin the right side of the sleeve to the right side of the dress, matching the pin at the top of the sleeve with the shoulder seam, and pin in position. Pull up the gathering threads so the top of the sleeve fits the top of the armhole. Pin the flat underarm part of the sleeve in position. Stitch. Press the seams open. Repeat with the other sleeve.

6 INSERT THE INVISIBLE ZIPPER
Position the zipper in the left side seam between the front and back, so the top of the teeth align with the sleeve hem edge. Insert the zipper following the instructions on pages 228–229. Stitch the seam from the bottom of the zipper to the hemline and press the seam open. To neaten the ends of the zipper tapes, fold the tops under and slipstitch in place.

7 STITCH THE RIGHT SIDE SEAM
Now stitch the right side seam from the hem, all the way up the side and along the short length of the underarm sleeve seam. Press the seam open.

8 HEM THE DRESS AND SEW ON THE BUTTONS
At the hemline, turn up and machine stitch a ⅜" (1 cm) double hem. Then sew two buttons to the dress front just below each shoulder seam.

GIRL'S DRESS

Parents love to see their daughters in pretty dresses, so imagine the sense of pride if you have made that dress yourself. Sewing children's clothing is a great way to practice techniques without wasting too much fabric if it goes wrong.

DIFFICULTY RATING: ⊞ ⊞ ⊞ ⊞ ⊞

Materials

I yd (90 cm) of a cotton print, 54" (137 cm) wide, OR

I²⁄₃ yd (1.4 m) of a cotton print, 45" (115 cm) wide

1½ yd (1.3 m) of contrasting double satin ribbon, 1³⁄₈" (3.5 cm) wide, for waist trim and bow (bow is optional)

2¼ yd (2 m) of decorative brocade ribbon with a scalloped edge, ³⁄₄" (2 cm) wide, for straps and hem edging

White tulle, enough to make a strip 2¼" (6 cm) wide by 3⅓ yd (3 m) long, for hem edging

Matching invisible zipper, 6½" (16 cm) long

Three button molds, for ½" (12 mm) covered buttons (optional)

Sewing thread to match fabric and ribbon

With no sleeves to set in and pretty jacquard ribbon used as straps, this dress is not only easy to make, but can "grow" with your child. Cut the straps a little long and leave the extra length behind the facing. If she's grown by next year, just undo a couple of stitches where it is sewn into the garment, lengthen the straps then re-sew. This design shows you the neatest way to add frills and ribbon to the hemline.

GIRL'S DRESS SIZES
To fit child 2–3 years, 4–5 years, 5–6 years, and 7–8 years.

FABRIC FINDER
Printed cottons like this are always a good choice as they look pretty and are easy to sew. You can create a completely different look by using an alternative but co-ordinated fabric for the bodice. *Try these alternatives:*
Gingham—Seersucker—Calico—Fine cotton lawn—Chambray

SKILLS SET
Working even slipstitch—page 208
Stitching straight seams—page 211 • Clipping curved seams—page 212 • Finishing seams—pages 214 and 215
Inserting an invisible zipper—pages 228 and 229

ENLARGE BY 500%

Pattern pieces

— SIZE 2–3 YEARS

— SIZE 4–5 YEARS

— SIZE 5–6 YEARS

— SIZE 7–8 YEARS

EACH SMALL GRAPH
SQUARE = ⅜" (1 CM)

**SKIRT FRONT AND
SKIRT BACK**
Cut 2 on the fold

BACK BODICE
Cut I on the fold

FRONT BODICE
Cut I on the fold

FRONT-BODICE FACING
Cut I on the fold

BACK-BODICE FACING
Cut I on the fold

Cutting diagram

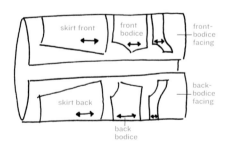

skirt front

front bodice

front-bodice facing

skirt back

back-bodice facing

back bodice

Cutting guide

Press the fabric thoroughly before cutting.

FROM THE FABRIC:

✄ Cut two skirts, one front bodice, one back bodice, one front-bodice facing, and one back-bodice facing, each on the fold.

A ⅝" (1.5 cm) seam allowance is included on all the pattern pieces, and a 1¼" (3 cm) hem allowance on the skirt front and back.

102

To make the girl's dress

1 STITCH THE BODICE PIECES TO THE SKIRT PIECES
With right sides together, stitch the bodice front to the skirt front and the bodice back to the skirt back. Finish the raw seam edges and press the seams open.

2 STITCH THE RIGHT SIDE SEAM
With right sides together, stitch the right dress side seam. Finish the raw seam edges and press the seams open.

3 STITCH ON THE SATIN RIBBON
Using tailor's chalk, and a steel ruler, mark a line ⅜" (1 cm) above and 1" (2.5 cm) below the waist seamline on the right side of the dress. Using these guidelines, pin the ribbon to the waist, starting at the dress's left side seam, working across the back and around to the front until you get to the left side seam again. Baste and then, using a zipper foot, topstitch it in place as close to the edges of the ribbon as possible. Remove the basting.

4 STITCH ONE FACING SIDE SEAM
Place the front-bodice facing on the front bodice and the back-bodice facing on the back bodice, with right sides together. Then pin together the same facing side seam as the side seam that is stitched on the bodice, with right sides together. Take the facing off the bodice, and baste and stitch the pinned seam. Remove the basting and press the seam open.

5 STITCH ON THE FACINGS AND RIBBON STRAPS

Cut two pieces of the scallop-edged brocade ribbon for the shoulder straps, each measuring 12" (30 cm) long. Next, with right sides together, pin one end of each shoulder strap ⅝" (1.5 cm) from the top corners of the front bodice. Now pin the other ends of the straps to the back bodice so they each measure 7" (18 cm) long. Leave extra ribbon for future adjustments. With right sides together, lay the prepared facing on top of the bodice over the straps. Starting and ending at the open side seam, stitch the facing in place along the armhole and neck edges. Snip the corners and clip the curves. Press the seams open, then press the facings to the inside of the dress and press the folded seam edge.

6 INSERT THE ZIPPER

On the left side seam, mark the end of the zipper position with a pin. Insert the invisible zipper and stitch the side seam. Take care to stitch the zipper to the dress only and leave the facing free. Press the seam open.

7 SLIPSTITCH THE FACING ENDS

Turn in one end of the facing at the zipper and slipstitch it to the zipper tape to finish. Repeat with the other end.

8 TURN UP THE HEM EDGE

Press ⅜" (1 cm) to the wrong side along the hem edge. Machine stitch this turning in place.

9 PREPARE THE RIBBON AND TULLE EDGING

Cut a length of decorative scallop-edged brocade ribbon 2" (5 cm) longer than the hem edge of the dress. Next, cut a 3¼ yd (3 m) length of tulle 2¼" (6 cm) wide and run gathering stitches along one long side, ¼" (6 mm) from one edge. Pin the gathered tulle to the top edge of the wrong side of the ribbon, positioning the line of gathering stitches ⅛" (3 mm) below the top edge of the ribbon. Then baste and stitch the tulle to the ribbon ⅛" (3 mm) from the top edge of the ribbon.

10 STITCH THE EDGING TO THE DRESS

With the dress right side out, lay it upside down so the hem edge is at the top. Starting at one side seam, pin the prepared ribbon-and-tulle edging right side down on the right side of the skirt, with the gathered edge of the tulle at the top and the center of the ribbon precisely ¾" (2 cm) from the hemline edge. When the edging is pinned in position, turn in the ends so they align with the seam and stitch them together. Machine stitch the edging in place, stitching exactly ¾" (2 cm) from the hem edge (along the center of the ribbon).

11 COMPLETE THE HEM

Fold the hem to the wrong side along the edging seam, so half the scalloped ribbon and the tulle frill peek out below the hem. Machine stitch the turned-up hem. Press, avoiding the tulle.

12 MAKE THE BOW

To make the decorative double bow for the center front of the dress, cut two lengths of satin ribbon, one 6" (15 cm) long and one 7½" (19 cm) long. Overlap the end of the shortest ribbon by ½" (1 cm) and hand sew the overlap together with a couple of stitches. Pinch this ring of ribbon together at the center, with the overlap at the center of one side and stitch it together with a couple of hand stitches to form a 2¾" (7 cm) bow. Make a 3½" (9 cm) bow in the same way with the longer length of ribbon. Place the shorter bow on top of the longer bow, wrap the bow center with a short length of ribbon and sew this length together on the wrong side of the bow. Stitch the bow to the ribbon at the center front of the dress.

🪡 Try this...

As an alternative to the bow, you could decorate the front bodice with three little fabric-covered buttons. Cover the buttons with the dress fabric, then sew them to the bodice front in a little line, between the neck edge and the satin ribbon.

TIE PILLOW

With no zippers or buttonholes, this pillow is one of the easiest makes in the book. Choosing a contrast lining and ties adds style to this otherwise plain pillow. With this simple design, it's possible to create an entire set of pillows in an afternoon.

DIFFICULTY RATING: ⊞ ⊞ ⊞ ⊞ ⊞

Super simple to make, if you can stitch in a straight line, you'll be able to make this elegant pillow cover with ties. There's no zipper to contend with and the ties are something of a trimming in themselves. The charm of the design lies in the flash of color from the lining, which can be seen due to the pillowcase-like construction of the cover. Aside from contrasting colors, the two fabrics used have contrasting textures as well—the outer fabric is a soft-to-the-touch furnishing fabric and the lining a shiny slubbed silk.

PILLOW SIZE
The finished pillow measures 17¾" x 17¾" (45 cm x 45 cm).

FABRIC FINDER
Scatter pillows can be made in almost any fabric, though furnishing fabrics are more durable and will withstand more wear and tear. The outside of this one is made from firm brushed upholstery cotton with a lining in slubbed silk.
Try these alternatives:

Furnishing cotton—Furnishing linen and linen blends—Linen blends—Furnishing silk—Jacquard—Duppioni—Tapestries—Chintz

Materials
- ⅔ yd (60 cm) of a medium-weight, closely woven fabric, at least 45" (115 cm) wide, for main fabric
- ½ yd (35 cm) of a raw silk, at least 44" (112 cm) wide, for lining fabric
- Matching sewing thread
- Pillow form to fit finished cover

SKILLS SET
Stitching straight seams—**page 211** • Finishing seams—**pages 214 and 215**

Cutting guide

Press the fabric thoroughly before cutting. Measure and mark the fabric carefully using a steel ruler and ensure all the corners are at perfect right angles before cutting.

FROM THE MAIN FABRIC:

✂ Cut one outer cover piece, measuring 36½" x 18¾" (92 cm x 47cm).

✂ Cut four strips for the ties, each 2½" x 10½" (6 cm x 26.5 cm).

FROM THE CONTRASTING LINING FABRIC:

✂ Cut two lining pieces, each 10¼" x 18¾" (25 cm x 47 cm).

✂ Cut four strips for the ties, each 2½" x 10½" (6 cm x 26.5 cm).

To make the tie pillow

1 PREPARE THE TIES

With right sides together, place a lining-fabric tie strip on top of a main-fabric tie strip, then snip off a 45-degree triangle of fabric right at one end of the strips. Pin the strips together, then machine stitch up one long edge, along the diagonal and down the other long edge, using a ⅜" (1 cm) seam allowance. Leave the straight end unstitched. Snip off the angled point, being careful not to cut the stitches. Press the seams open, turn right side out, and press again. Prepare the remaining three ties in the same way. Be sure to shape the tie ends in the same way so the angled ends all slant in the same direction.

2 PREPARE THE LINING PIECES

Along one long side of each lining piece, fold under ⅜" (1 cm) twice and press to form a double hem. Machine stitch the hem in place close to the first fold.

3 STITCH ON THE LINING PIECES

Lay the main fabric piece right side up on a flat surface. On the short ends of the piece, measure and mark with pins the positions for the ties, centered and 4¼" (11 cm) apart. Pin the ties in place, with the main fabric on the ties facing the main fabric piece and with the raw edges aligned. With the right sides together, place a lining piece on top of the ties at each end of the main piece. Using a ⅜" (1 cm) seam allowance, stitch through all layers, so catching in the ties. Press the seams open. If you think the raw edges of your fabrics will unravel easily, finish the raw edges of the seams you have just stitched.

4 STITCH SIDE SEAMS

Fold the whole piece in half widthwise, aligning the lining seams, and pin and stitch all along both side seams, again taking a ⅜" (1 cm) seam. Press the seams open.

5 ADD THE FINISHING TOUCHES

Finish the raw edges of the side seams if desired. Then turn the cover right side out and push the lining inside the cover. Press thoroughly. Put the pillow form in the cover, tucking it under one side of the lining—just like you would in a pillowcase. Lastly, tie the ties neatly together.

COOK'S APRON

Easy to sew, aprons are often the first projects taught at beginners' classes. With no difficult fastenings or shapings to deal with—only straight seams, gathering, and ties—an apron affords plenty of practice with basic sewing skills.

DIFFICULTY RATING: ⊞ ⊞ ⊞ ⊞ ⊞

Materials

⅞ yd (70 cm) of a cotton duck print, 54″ (137 cm) wide, for main fabric

½ yd (40 cm) of a contrasting plain cotton duck, 54″ (137 cm) wide, for neck straps, waistband, waist ties, and ruffle

16″ x 24″ (40 cm x 60 cm) of a cotton lining fabric

3 yd (2.7 m) of ready-made bias binding, ½″ (12 mm) wide

Matching sewing thread

T his apron is almost a sampler of key sewing skills—gathering, putting on a waistband, making a lined bib, even adding ruffles and bias binding. But as it's essentially flat with no complicated shaping or fastenings, there's little to go wrong. This project makes a great homemade gift for cook's of all ages.

APRON SIZE
The finished apron is approximately 35½″ (90 cm) long, from the top of the bib to the bottom of the ruffle.

FABRIC FINDER
The cotton duck used for this apron is a medium-weight canvas-type fabric. It is closely woven: good for protecting clothing from oily cooking splashes.
Try these alternatives:
Gingham—Cotton prints—Calico—Chambray

SKILLS SET
Working even slipstitch—page 208 • Stitching straight seams—page 211
Clipping curved seams—page 212 • Finishing seams—pages 214 and 215
Hand gathering—page 222 • Applying bias binding—page 231

ENLARGE
BY 500%

Pattern pieces

EACH SMALL GRAPH SQUARE = ³⁄₈" (I CM)

SKIRT
Cut I on the fold

BIB LINING
Cut I on the fold

WAISTBAND
Cut I on the fold

BIB
Cut I on the fold

112

Cutting diagrams

LINING FABRIC

bib lining

waistband

CONTRASTING FABRIC

bib

skirt

MAIN FABRIC

Cutting guide

Press the fabric thoroughly before cutting.

FROM THE MAIN FABRIC:

✂ Cut one skirt and one bib, both on the fold.

FROM THE CONTRASTING FABRIC:

✂ Cut one waistband, on the fold.

✂ Cut one strip for the ruffle, measuring 2⅜" x 54" (6 cm x 137 cm).

✂ Cut two strips for the waist ties, each 3¼" x 33" (8 cm x 84 cm), and two strips for the neck straps, each 3¼" x 22¾" (8 cm x 58 cm).

FROM THE LINING FABRIC:

✂ Cut one bib lining, on the fold.

A ⅜" (1 cm) seam allowance is included on all the pattern pieces.

To make the apron

1 PREPARE THE NECK STRAPS AND WAIST TIES
Fold one of the waist ties in half lengthwise and press. Trim one end of the folded strip at a 45-degree angle to create a diagonal end. Using a ⅜" (1 cm) seam allowance, stitch along the long edge and the diagonal end, leaving the straight end of the tie open. Clip off the point of the seam allowance at the shaped end and turn the tie right side out. Prepare the remaining waist tie and both neck straps in the same way.

2 SEW THE WAISTBAND TO THE BIB
With right sides together, stitch the waistband to the lower edge of the bib. Press the seam open, then press it away from the bib. It is important to press the seam downward so it isn't in the way of the lining seam in the next step.

3 LINE THE BIB

Place the bib right side up on a flat surface. With raw edges aligned, pin a neck strap just inside the seam allowance at either side of the top edge of the bib. Now lay the bib lining right side down on top of the straps and pin, aligning the edges with the bib piece below. Stitch through all layers along the top and from the top down to the waistband on each side. Be sure to stitch right up to the waistband seam, but do not stitch into the waistband. Clip off the corners and trim the seams. Press the seams open and turn right side out.

4 SEW ON THE WAIST TIES

At one end of the waistband, pin one waist tie to the side edge of the waistband, with right sides together and with the tie seam facing downward. Stitch the tie to the waistband—make sure this seam is aligned with the end of the bib-and-lining seam. Press the seam toward the waistband. Repeat with the other waist tie. Leave the lining loose at the waist, it will be slipstitched in place after the skirt is added on.

5 STITCH ON THE SKIRT RUFFLE

At the hem edge, with right sides together, pin the contrasting ruffle strip to the apron skirt, making even pleats about 1½" (4 cm) wide with a ⅜" (1 cm) return. Take your time and adjust the pleats until you're happy they're as even as possible—they don't have to be perfect. Baste the ruffle in place, then stitch ⅜" (1 cm) from the edge. Remove the basting and press the seam toward the skirt. To neaten the seam, finish the raw edges with machine zigzag or overlocking stitches.

6 BIND THE EDGES OF THE SKIRT AND RUFFLE
Next, cover the raw edges of the ruffle and the side edges of the skirt with ready-made bias binding. Starting at one side edge of the skirt, pin and baste the binding in place down the side of the skirt, along the side of the ruffle, across the bottom of the ruffle, and up the other side of the ruffle and skirt. Stitch the binding close to its edge. Remove the basting and press.

7 SEW THE BIB AND SKIRT TOGETHER
Run gathering stitches along 13½" (34 cm) at the center of the top edge of the skirt. With right sides together, pin the skirt to the lower edge of the waistband, drawing the gathers up to fit the waistband. Baste and stitch. Remove the basting and press the seam upward.

8 SLIPSTITCH THE LINING IN PLACE
On the reverse, turn in the raw edges of the lining where the waist ties are stitched on. Then turn in the raw edge along the bottom of the lining, aligning the fold with the bottom of the waistband and pin. Slipstitch all along to finish.

PROM DRESS

This 1950s-inspired dress with its simple halter neckline, takes on the style of a classic prom dress. Having mastered the art of boning, you'll be able to tackle any special occasion outfit. Make the dress in spotted cotton for everyday wear or satin for evening wear or a bridesmaid's dress.

DIFFICULTY RATING: ⊞ ⊞ ⊞ ⊞ ⊡

Making a boned bodice might be daunting, but if you take your time and follow the steps, it's surprisingly easy and ultimately very satisfying. The trick is to make sure you seam the pieces together accurately, in the right order and the right way up. This boned bodice has been designed with relatively few pieces so even beginners can get to grips with the method without going wrong.

PROM DRESS SIZES
To fit women's sizes 6, 8, 10, 12, and 14.

FABRIC FINDER
A crisp cotton with a navy ground and white polka dots was chosen for this dress. Fabric with a little body gives the circular skirt a stand-out flare, but a more flimsy or more slinky fabric would suit the design just as well. You could make your first version in cotton and progress to silk for the next.
Try these alternatives:
Fine cotton prints—Raw silk—Silky crepe—Fine jersey

Materials
2⅔ yd (2.4 m) of a print, 54" (137 cm) wide, OR
3¾ yd (3.4 m) of a print, 45" (115 cm) wide
24" x 28" (60 cm x 70 cm) of woven iron-on interfacing
1½ yd (1.5 m) of cotton-covered boning
1⅓ yd (1.2 m) of grosgrain ribbon, 1¼" (3 cm) wide, for the belt
Matching invisible zipper, 18" (46 cm) long
Matching sewing thread

SKILLS SET
Working even slipstitching—**page 208** • Slipstitching double-fold hems—**page 210**
Stitching straight seams—**page 211** • Clipping curved seams—**page 212**
Finishing seams—**pages 214 and 215** • Inserting an invisible zipper—**pages 228 and 229**

HALTERNECK STRAP
Cut 2 on the fold

SIZE 6
SIZE 8
SIZE 10
SIZE 12
SIZE 14

EACH SMALL GRAPH
SQUARE = ⅜" (1 CM)

BACK-NECK FACING
Cut 1 on the fold

SKIRT FRONT AND
SKIRT BACK
Cut 2 on the fold

ENLARGE
BY 500%

Pattern pieces

FRONT-NECK FACING
Cut 1 on the fold

CENTER FRONT BODICE
Cut 1 on the fold

BACK BODICE SIDE
Cut 2

FRONT
BODICE
SIDE
Cut 2

CENTER
BACK
BODICE
Cut 1 on
the fold

Cutting diagrams

skirt front

skirt back

MAIN FABRIC

center front bodice

center back bodice

back-neck facing

strap

front bodice side

back bodice side

front-neck facing

MAIN FABRIC

MAIN FABRIC FUSED WITH INTERFACING

Cutting guide

Press the fabric thoroughly before cutting.

FROM THE FABRIC:

✄ Cut two skirts, one back-neck facing, one front-neck facing, and two halterneck straps, each on the fold.

FROM THE FABRIC FUSED WITH INTERFACING:

Press the iron-on interfacing onto the wrong side of a piece of fabric measuring 24" x 28" (60 cm x 70 cm). Then fold this interfaced piece in half widthwise.

✄ Cut one center front bodice and one center back bodice, both on the fold.

✄ Cut two back bodice sides and two front bodice sides.

A ⅝" (1.5 cm) seam allowance and a 2" (5 cm) hem allowance are included on the pattern pieces.

To make the prom dress

1 PREPARE THE HALTERNECK STRAP

With right sides together, match the two halterneck strap pieces. Stitch along the long edges, leaving the ends open. Trim the seams and clip the curves. Turn the strap right side out and press.

2 PREPARE THE FRONT AND BACK BODICE

With right sides together, stitch the left front bodice to the center front bodice and then the right front bodice to the center front bodice. Repeat this process with the back bodice pieces. To prepare for boning, press the seams open using plenty of pressure and steam. For boning, it is important seams are pressed fully open and flat.

3 ADD THE BONING TO FRONT AND BACK BODICE

Cut a piece of boning to the length of each seam just stitched, then snip 1½" (4 cm) off one end of each (this is to allow for seam allowances). Pin and baste the boning to the seam allowances, ensuring each piece lies just short of the seam allowance at the top and bottom of the seam. The boning is stitched to the seam allowances so the stitching lines do not show on the right side of the dress. Use a zipper foot to stitch as close as possible to each boning edge.

4 STITCH THE BODICE AND THE SKIRT
With right sides together, stitch the front bodice and back bodice together along the right side seam. In the same way, stitch the right side seam of the skirt. Press the seams open.

5 JOIN THE BODICE TO THE SKIRT
With right sides together and raw edges meeting, stitch the skirt to the bodice, matching the side seam of the bodice to the side seam of the skirt. Press the seam open, then press it upward. Finish the raw edges.

6 INSERT THE ZIPPER AND SEW THE HEM
Insert the invisible zipper into the left side seam of the dress, then stitch the remaining seam from the bottom of the zipper to the hemline. Turn up and stitch a 1" (2.5 cm) double hem.

7 SEW ON THE NECK FACING AND STRAP
With right sides together, stitch the front and back neck facing pieces together along the right side seam. Press the seam open. Turn up and press ⅜" (1 cm) along the lower edge of facing. Stitch in place. With raw edges aligned, pin the halterneck strap to the right side of the bodice, so the inside strap seam aligns on either side with the outside center front seams of the bodice. Now place the prepared facing right side down top of this, matching the right side seam and the curved edges of the front. Pin, baste, and stitch. Trim the seams and press open. Fold the facing to the inside, then turn in the raw edges at each end of the facing and slipstitch close to the zipper.

8 STITCH ON THE BELT
Cut the grosgrain to fit the waistline, plus extra for turning under ⅜" (1 cm) at each end. Turn under ⅜" (1 cm) at each end and pin in position exactly over the waist seam. Hand stitch in place along the short ends using slipstitches—leave the rest of the ribbon loose around the waist.

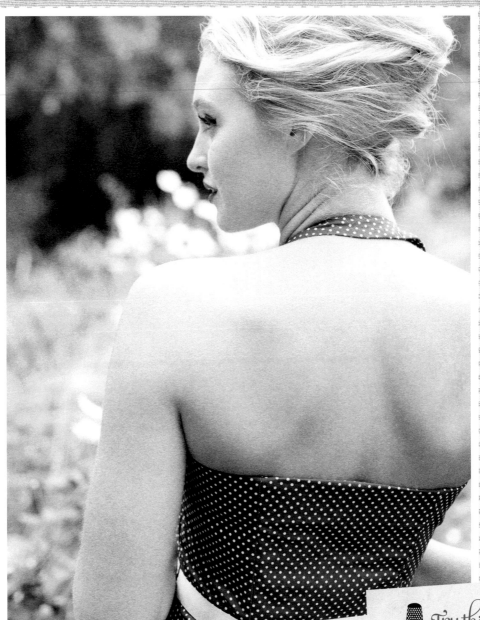

Try this...

For a neater finish, remove the boning from its casing before stitching. This makes it much easier to get the stitching straight. Once the casing is in position, just slip the boning back in.

WINDOW PANEL

This simple, chic window treatment can be made in sheer white or a bright organza. It's the project to choose if you're meticulous by nature but new to sewing. With a flat panel, you'll get plenty of straight sewing practice, but you must be precise in the cutting.

DIFFICULTY RATING: ⊞ ⊞ ⊞ ⊞ ⊞

Materials

Sheer linen to fit your window (see the Cutting Guide for how much fabric to purchase)

Striped grosgrain ribbon, 1″ (2.5 cm) wide and as long as the width of the finished window panel plus 1¼″ (3 cm)

Matching sewing thread

Plastic-covered curtain tensile wire with metal eyes and two metal hooks, as long as the width of the window

Round wooden dowel, ½″ (12 mm) in diameter and as long as the width of the finished window panel (optional)

M aking a sheer panel couldn't be easier as there's no lining or gathering to contend with. However, to make it look smart, you need to be meticulous about how you cut out the fabric, making sure it is absolutely square. A ribbon trimming can be added to the bottom edge, like the one shown here, or it can be left plain. However, a line of trimming provides extra weight and rigidity to keep the panel in shape.

WINDOW PANEL SIZE
The window panel can be made to fit any window size.

FABRIC FINDER
This panel is made in pure cotton voile. Aim to choose a sheer that has some body to it. Synthetics are inclined to be more floppy than natural fibers and are more suited to sheers that are gathered.
Try these alternatives:
Cotton organdy—Sheer linen—Furnishing silk organza

SKILLS SET
Slipstitching double-fold hems—**page 210**

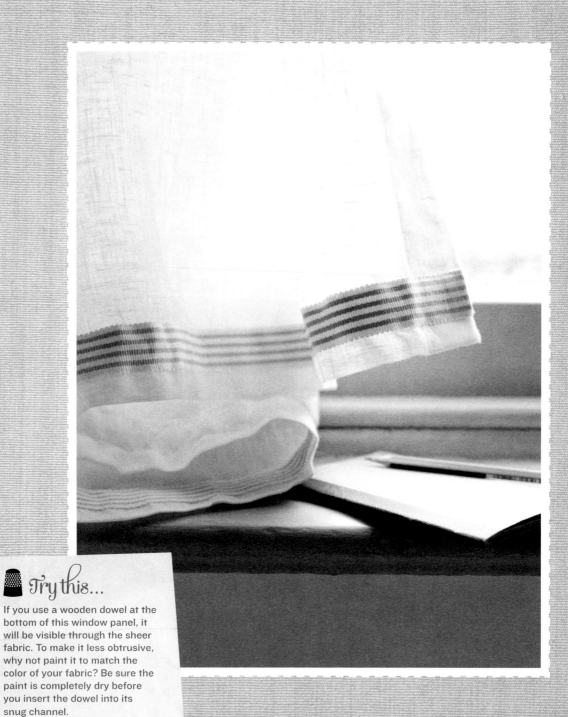

🪡 Try this...

If you use a wooden dowel at the bottom of this window panel, it will be visible through the sheer fabric. To make it less obtrusive, why not paint it to match the color of your fabric? Be sure the paint is completely dry before you insert the dowel into its snug channel.

Cutting guide

FROM THE CURTAIN FABRIC:

✂ Cut a piece of fabric that is 6" (16 cm) longer and wider than the size of the finished window panel. Sheer fabric is difficult to cut in a straight line, so for really straight edges, first cut the fabric piece ¾" (2 cm) longer and ¾" (2 cm) wider than the dimensions you have just calculated for your piece of fabric. Then trim it down to the correct size. To do this, carefully pull out one thread along each edge to give you an accurate straight edge. Cut the excess off the frayed edges until you have the exact measurements for the panel.

To make the window panel,

1 HEM THE TOP, BOTTOM, AND SIDES OF THE PANEL

Fold and press 1½" (4 cm) to the wrong side along one vertical edge of the panel, measuring the turning every 4" (10 cm) for accuracy. Press 1½" (4 cm) to the wrong side again so you have a double hem, and pin. Topstitch the hem ⅛" (3 mm) from the first fold, being careful to keep the stitching really straight. Repeat along the other vertical edge. Stitch a 1½" (4 cm) double hem along the top and bottom of the panel in the same way for a perfectly formed rectangle.

2 CREATE A CHANNEL FOR THE TENSILE WIRE

Add an additional line of stitching along the center of the hem at the top of the panel, ¾" (2 cm) from the top folded edge. This creates a channel below the new line of stitching for the tensile wire.

3 SEW ON THE RIBBON TRIM

Pin the grosgrain ribbon to the right side of the window panel along the bottom hem, aligning the top of the ribbon with the top of the hem. At each end of the ribbon, fold ⅝" (1.5 cm) into the inside of the hem. Using a zipper foot, stitch the ribbon in place along the top and bottom edges, as close to the edge as possible. This creates a channel in the bottom hem for the wooden dowel if you are using one to weight the panel.

4 HANG THE FINISHED PANEL

Thread the covered tensile wire through the channel created for it at the top of the panel. Screw a screw eye into each end. Screw a hook into the architrave ¾" (2 cm) from the top of the window frame so that it is in line with where the tensile wire sits inside the panel channel. Then hang the window panel in position.

5 INSERT THE DOWEL

To weight the panel, slide the wooden dowel into the channel behind the ribbon. There's no need to stitch up the ends as it's unlikely to slip out, yet it can easily be removed when you want to launder the panel.

HACKING JACKET

This classic tweed hacking jacket is a complex project that novice sewers will need to work up to. However, once you have made your own jacket, tailored for a perfect fit, you'll never want to buy one off-the-peg ever again.

DIFFICULTY RATING: ⊞ ⊞ ⊞ ⊞ ⊞

Materials

2¼ yd (2 m) of a wool fabric, 60" (150 cm) wide, for main jacket fabric

¼ yd (20 cm) of a lightweight contrasting fabric (such as a satin suit-lining fabric), 45" (115 cm) wide, for fold-back cuffs

2¼ yd (2 m) of medium-weight iron-on interfacing, 20–25" (50–64 cm) wide

One button, 1" (2.5 cm) in diameter

Tailored jackets are not a good choice for beginners. Negotiating the notched lapel and setting in the sleeves smoothly are tasks that require accurate stitching and plenty of experience easing fabric. That said, once you do have sewing experience, making your own jacket gives you the opportunity to make-it-to-perfect-measure. If you were to do this, it's best to follow the example of bespoke tailors and make one up in a toile (calico) to begin with so you can try it on and make adjustments before cutting the fabric. This New Look pattern for an unlined jacket is easier to make than a lined one, but add flair with the cute contrasting cuffs.

FABRIC FINDER

This jacket is made in a tweedy wool, perfect for tailoring as it takes shape well and doesn't crease too easily.
Try these alternatives:
Wool—Worsted—Linen—Heavy cotton—Gabardine

SKILLS SET

Working even slipstitch—**page 208** • Stitching straight seams—**page 211**
Clipping curved seams—**page 212** • Finishing seams—**pages 214 and 215**
Grading seams—**page 218** • Making single-point darts—**page 220**
Easing—**page 223** • Making buttonholes—**page 232** • Adding buttons—**page 233**

UNDERCOLLAR
Cut 2

FRONT
Cut 2

BACK
Cut I on the fold

SIZE 6
SIZE 8
SIZE IO
SIZE I2
SIZE I4

EACH SMALL GRAPH
SQUARE = $\frac{3}{8}$" (I CM)

SIDE FRONT
Cut 2

SIDE BACK
Cut 2

BACK FACING
Cut I on the fold

FRONT FACING
Cut 2

SLEEVE FACING
Cut 2

SLEEVE
Cut 2

POCKET
Cut 1 or 2

UPPER COLLAR
Cut 1 on the fold

Pattern pieces

ENLARGE
BY 500%

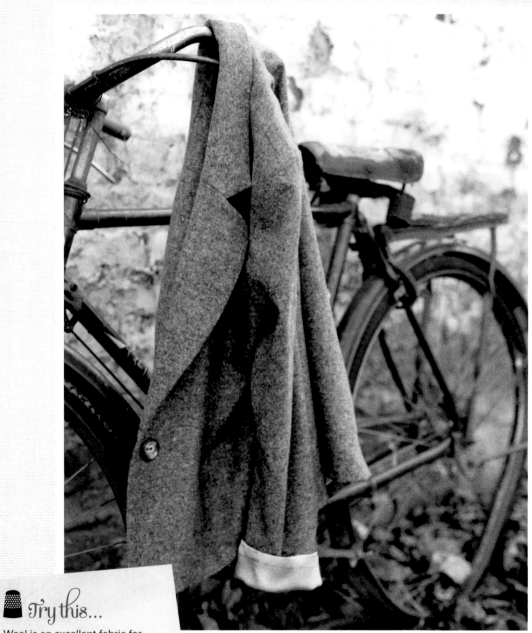

Try this…

Wool is an excellent fabric for
tailoring as it can be steamed
into shape. When you have set in
the sleeves, put the shoulders over
the end of the ironing board and
press the armhole sleeves well,
using plenty of steam to help the
stitches settle into the fabric.

Cutting guide

Press the fabric thoroughly before cutting.

FROM THE MAIN FABRIC:

✄ Cut two fronts, two side fronts, two side backs, two undercollars, two front facings, two sleeves, and one or two pockets (as preferred).

✄ Cut one center back, one upper collar, and one back facing, each on the fold.

FROM THE CONTRASTING FABRIC:

✄ Cut two sleeve facings for the lower end of each sleeve.

FROM THE INTERFACING:

✄ Cut two sleeve facings, two undercollars, and two front facings.

✄ Cut one upper collar and one back facing, both on the fold. Following the manufacturer's instructions, iron the interfacing onto the wrong side of the relevant pieces.

A ⅝" (1.5 cm) seam allowance and all hem allowances are included on the pattern pieces.

Cutting diagram

To make the jacket

1 STITCH TOGETHER THE FRONT AND BACK PIECES
With right sides together, stitch the back side pieces to the center back and one front side piece to each front piece. Press the front seams toward the center front edges and the back seams toward the center back. Then stitch the back and front together along the shoulder and side seams. Press these seams open. Finish the raw seam edges as desired.

2 PREPARE THE POCKET
At the upper edge of the pocket, press ¼" (6 mm) to the wrong side. Turn this upper edge to the outside along the foldline—about 1¼" (3 cm) from the first fold—to form a facing. Stitch around the outer edge of the sides and bottom of the pocket, stitching along the seamline and over the facing at each end. Trim off the corner at the facing. Make a line of gathering stitches inside the seam allowance all along the pocket edge. Turn the facing to the wrong side and press. Topstitch along the top of the pocket, close to the first hem fold. Fold the seam allowance to the wrong side along the seamline stitching, pulling up the gathering stitches to ease the fabric at the corners, and pin. Clip the curves where the easing stitches have created fullness. Baste. If you are adding two pockets, do the same with the second pocket.

3 STITCH ON THE POCKET
Pin the pocket to the front of the jacket, matching the marks. Topstitch down one side, along the bottom and up the other side of the pocket. Alternatively, slipstitch the pocket in place. If you have a second pocket, repeat.

4 STITCH THE ENDS OF THE UNDERCOLLAR TO THE LAPELS
Stitch the center back seam of the undercollar. Press the seam open. With right sides together, pin the ends of the undercollar to the front neck edge along the lapel, matching the large and small dots. Stitch between the large and small dots. Clip the front to the large dot, taking care not to cut any stitches, and grade the seam.

5 STITCH THE NECK EDGE AND MAKE THE DARTS
Baste the neck-edge dart on each front. Then, with right sides together, pin the rest of the undercollar to the jacket, matching the notches. Stitch from the center back along the stitching line to the point of one dart. Return to the center back and stitch along the stitching line to the point of the other dart.

6 PREPARE THE JACKET FACING
Make a line of staystitches along the neck edge of the back facing and between the dots on the lapel edge of the front facings. Stitch the facing sections together at the shoulder seams. Press the seams open. Press ⅜" (1 cm) to the wrong side on the inner edges of the front facing and the lower edge of the back facing. Stitch. On the front facing, clip the front facing at the large dot and small dot, being careful not to cut into the staystitching.

7 STITCH THE UPPER COLLAR TO THE FACING
With right sides together, pin the upper collar to the neck edge of the facing, matching the large and small dots and matching the remaining small dots to the shoulder seams. Stitch between the large dots and layer the seams. Press the seams open.

8 STITCH THE UPPER COLLAR AND FACING TO THE JACKET

With right sides together, pin the upper collar and facing to the undercollar and jacket, matching the center back and the large and small dots. You will need to ease the upper collar and facing to fit by pulling it in place as you go and break the stitch at the large dot. Baste and stitch. Grade the seam.

9 FINISH THE HEM AND BODY

Turn the facing to the inside and press. You'll find as you do this, the hem will turn up to the correct length where the facing is sewn onto the front of the jacket. Press the hem up at this level and press in the raw edge by ⅝" (1.5 cm) and hand stitch the hem. Lift up the back facing and slipstitch the neck seam allowances together.

10 PREPARE THE SLEEVES

Run gathering stitches along the sleeve head between the notches. With right sides together, stitch the sleeve seam. Press the seam open. With right sides together, stitch the sleeve facing seams, to form tubes. Press the seams open. With right sides together, pin the raw edge of the facing to the lower edge of the sleeve, matching the seams. Baste and stitch. Press the seam away from the sleeve. On the sleeve facing, press a ⅜" (1 cm) hem to the wrong side and stitch. Press the facing to the inside of the sleeve and hand stitch the top edge in place.

11 SET IN THE SLEEVES

Turn the jacket inside out and the sleeve right side out. Put the sleeve into the armhole, matching the small dot with the shoulder seam and matching the underarm seam. Baste the lower part of the sleeve into the armhole position between the notches. At the top of the sleeve, pull up the easing stitches to fit the armhole and distribute the fullness evenly. Baste and stitch. Trim the seam and press the seam allowance to shrink the fullness.

12 ADD THE BUTTONHOLE AND BUTTON

The only finishing touch left is to work the buttonhole on the right front and sew the button to the left front.

BOW TIE

*Bow ties don't have to be black or white—
here's your chance to add a splash of color to
any outfit. This one is made in slubbed silk,
which presses up smartly and comes
in an endless range of hues.*

DIFFICULTY RATING: ● ⊞ ⊞ ⊞ ⊞

Materials

12" x 44" (30 cm x 110 cm)
  of a slubbed silk
8" x 36" (20 cm x
  90 cm) of fine iron-on
  interfacing
Matching sewing thread
Metal bow-tie hook,
  eye, and adjustment
  slider, with ¾" (19 mm)
  wide slots

Making a comeback, bow ties are a smart retro accessory. They really aren't difficult to make and once you've perfected the techniques to make perfect curves, points, and corners, you'll want to be making them by the dozen for all the boys in your life. Using very little fabric, they don't cost a lot to make, so they're also an excellent accessory to sew in bulk for school fundraisers.

BOW TIE SIZE
The tie is made in two pieces and the length is adjustable. Each of the two finished tie pieces measures approximately 2¾" (7 cm) across the widest end and ¾" (2 cm) across the narrowest end.

FABRIC FINDER
Bow ties are traditionally made in pure silk, but any fine fabric that doesn't crease too readily will work as long as it's first backed with interfacing.
Try these alternatives:
Smooth lightweight silk—Lightweight silk prints—Raw silk—
Fine close-weave cotton

SKILLS SET
Working even slipstitch—**page 208** • Stitching straight seams—**page 211**
Clipping curved seams—**page 212**

EACH SMALL GRAPH SQUARE = ⅜" (1 CM)

Cutting guide

Press the fabric thoroughly, aligning the threads so warp and weft are as straight as possible before cutting.

FROM THE MAIN FABRIC:

✂ Cut one short tie piece and one long tie piece.

FROM THE MAIN FABRIC WITH INTERFACING:

✂ Iron the interfacing onto the wrong side of the remaining fabric, then cut one short tie piece and one long tie piece.

A ⅜" (1 cm) seam allowance is included on the bow tie pieces.

 Try this...

Firmly press the bow tie at all the early stages while it is inside out. Once it is turned through, instead of pressing hard, hover the iron over the bow tie and give it several good shots of steam. This avoids the ridges of the seam allowances showing through.

To make the bow tie

1 STITCH THE TIE PIECES TOGETHER

Place the short tie pieces right sides together. Stitch, taking a ⅜" (1 cm) seam allowance and leaving an 3" (8 cm) gap in the seam along one side of the narrow strip—this is for turning the piece right side out. Keep the ⅜" (1 cm) seam width consistent all around the curves, the corners and the point to ensure a neatly shaped tie. Press the seams flat to embed the stitches. Snip off the corners of the seam allowances and clip the curves, taking care not to cut into any of the stitching lines. Stitch and trim the long tie pieces in exactly the same way.

2 COMPLETE THE TWO TIE PIECES

Turn the short and long tie pieces right side out through the opening in the seam. Fold in the seam allowances along the opening and slipstitch the sides of the opening together to close it. Press.

3 ADD ON THE TIE HOOK

Thread the narrow pointed end of the short tie piece through the metal bow-tie hook and fold about 1½" (4 cm) of this tie end onto the reverse side of the tie. Slipstitch the pointed end in place.

4 ADD ON THE EYE AND SLIDER

Thread the narrow pointed end of the long tie piece through the slider and then the hook-eye. Now thread the end back around the slider bar in the opposite direction as shown and pin the end down on itself. Slide the slider up and down to check that it works, then slipstitch the pointed end in place.

To tie the bow tie

5 START TO TIE THE BOW TIE
The tie opens at the back, which means it is kept tied. To tie, first put the bow tie around your neck with the hook and eye at the back and bring the bow parts forward. Cross the right end over the left and then back up under it.

6 START FORMING THE BOW
Fold the left end of the bow tie to the left, then back to the right on top of itself.

7 COMPLETE THE BOW
Bring the right end down over the center, back up behind it, and over to the front again, then fold it in half as you push it through the center piece. Sounds complicated, but just think of it as tying a neat bow. Take the tie off by unclipping the hook.

Try this...

If you're new to machine stitching, or would like to perfect your skills, make a "test" bow tie using fabric from your scrap bag. You can leave out the interfacing on this first go.

CAMISOLE

A pretty camisole is a useful wardrobe basic. Team it with a skirt for evening, or give it a daytime look with a pair of jeans. By making your own, you can add quality details like mother-of-pearl buttons and lace edging.

DIFFICULTY RATING: ⊞ ⊞ ⊞ ⊞ ⊞

Materials

1¾ yd (1.5 m) of a silk crepe de Chine or other pure or fine synthetic silk, 45" (115 cm) wide

Matching sewing thread

Three mother-of-pearl buttons, ⅜" (1 cm) in diameter

1½ yd (1.3 m) of lace edging, about ⅝" (1.5 cm) wide, to trim the hem

The delightful pintucked detail on this pretty shell-pink satin camisole is surprisingly easy to achieve. Stitched on a square of satin, it is then cut to shape and stitched onto the main front piece before making up. Real silk satin garments like this are expensive to buy, yet easy to sew, and so are well worth making up at home.

CAMISOLE SIZES
To fit women's sizes 6, 8, 10, 12, and 14.

FABRIC FINDER
Pure silk is wonderful against the skin. It's cool in summer, yet provides surprising warmth in the winter when teamed with heavier daywear. Soft ballet-shoe pink is a romantic choice that works well with most other colors.
Try these alternatives:
Silk crepe de Chine—Synthetic silk—Synthetic crepe de Chine—Fine cotton lawn

SKILLS SET
Slipstitching double-fold hems—**page 210** • Stitching straight seams—**page 211**
Stitching French seams—**page 216** • Making and applying bias binding—**pages 230 and 231**

ENLARGE BY 500%

YOKE
Cut I on fold

SIZE 6
SIZE 8
SIZE 10
SIZE 12
SIZE 14

EACH SMALL GRAPH
SQUARE = ³⁄₈" (I CM)

FRONT
Cut I on fold

BACK
Cut I on fold

Cutting diagram

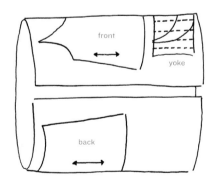

front

yoke

back

Cutting guide

Press the fabric thoroughly before cutting.

FROM THE FABRIC:

✄ Cut one camisole front and one camisole back, both on the fold.

A ⅝" (1.5 cm) seam allowance on the side seams and a ½" (12 mm) double hem allowance on the hem edges, the top back edge, and the front armhole edge are included on the pattern pieces. The front neck edge does not need a hem allowance as it is bound with a bias strip. Set aside the yoke pattern piece—the yoke is cut out from fabric after it is pintucked. The ¼" (6 mm) turn-under on the yoke outside curved edge is added when the piece is cut in step 3.

To make the camisole

1 MARK THE PINTUCKS ON THE YOKE

To prepare the pintucked yoke, cut a square of fabric 7" x 7" (18 cm x 18 cm). Using tailor's chalk, mark the positions of the pintucks on the right side of the fabric. Start by drawing two lines 1¼" (3 cm) apart at the center of the fabric, then draw two lines either side of these, each ⅝" (1.5 cm) from its neighbor. Alternatively, transfer the pintuck positions from the pattern piece onto the fabric.

2 STITCH THE PINTUCKS

Fold the fabric along one marked line and, using a zipper foot, stitch as close to the fold as you can. Press. Re-fold the fabric on the next line and stitch in the same way. Repeat for all the lines. Press the pintucks away from the center.

3 CUT OUT THE YOKE SHAPE

With wrong sides together, fold the pintucked fabric along the exact center between the two center pintucks. Place the yoke pattern piece on the fold over the prepared pintucks and cut out, adding an extra ¼" (6 mm) along the outside curved edge for a turn-under (but not along the neck edge).

4 STITCH ON THE YOKE

Press ¼" (6 mm) to the wrong side all around the outside curved edge of the prepared yoke and baste. Position the yoke right side up on top of the right side of the camisole front piece and baste in place. Topstitch around the curved edge, stitching as close as possible to the fold. Remove the basting. Stitch three buttons to the yoke between the center pintucks, the first 1" (2.5 cm) below the neck edge and the others ¾" (2 cm) apart below the first.

5 STITCH THE BACK AND FRONT TOGETHER

Join the side seams using the French seam method. To do this, first place the front piece on the back piece, with wrong sides together, and stitch the side seams ¼" (5 mm) from the edge. Press the seams open. Fold along the seamline so the front and back are positioned with right sides together. Stitch again, but this time ⅜" (1 cm) from the fold.

6 FINISH THE TOP, ARMHOLE, AND HEM EDGES

Stitch double-fold hems along the armhole and top back edges, and along the camisole hemline. For each of these hems, turn under ¼" (6 mm) twice, pin, and baste. Then stitch close to the first fold of the double-fold hem. (Remember to leave the front neck edge raw, as this will be covered with bias binding.)

7 STITCH ON THE HEM LACE

For a delicate detail, add some lace along the hemline. Starting at one side seam, pin the top edge of the lace edging behind the hemline. Hand sew the ends of the lace together where they meet. Baste the lace in place, then stitch close to the edge of the fabric using a zipper foot. Remove the basting.

8 CUT THE BIAS BINDING AND BIND THE NECK EDGE

From the fabric, cut enough 1" (2.5 cm) wide bias strips to piece together a continuous strip 1¾ yd (1.5 m) long. Make sure your strips are as long as possible and that one is at least 20" (50 cm) long. Stitch the pieces together to form the continous strip, using the longest strip at the center, and press the seams open. Fold the strip in half widthwise and mark the center point. With right sides together, pin this to the center front of the camisole. Baste from this point to the end of the camisole neck edge. Repeat on the other side. Stitch the binding to the neck edge, starting from the center in the same way and taking a ¼" (6 mm) seam allowance. Press in ¼" (6 mm) along the raw edge of the binding where it is stitched to the neck edge, fold to the inside of the camisole and pin. Slipstitch the binding in place along the neck-edge seamline.

9 FINISH THE STRAPS

Turn in and press ¼" (6 mm) along both raw edges, then pin together and baste. Using a zipper foot, stitch close to the edge. Put the camisole on, bring the straps over your shoulders, cross over and pin to the right length at the back. Stitch in position and trim the ends.

BOYFRIEND SHIRT

A boyfriend shirt is a great off-duty staple that can be worn buttoned up long and loose over leggings or open like a jacket with jeans. Learn to make your own and you'll benefit from endless fabric choices.

DIFFICULTY RATING: ⊞ ⊞ ⊞ ⊞ ⊞

C ollars, cuffs, sleeves, and button bands all contrive to make shirts something of a challenging project. But this is something of a cheat's shirt so you can achieve the look a little more easily. The yoke is simply applied on top of the main pattern piece—no lining and facing. The sleeves have turn-ups rather than tricky cuffs, while the buttonhole bands are attached like bias binding.

SHIRT SIZES
To fit women's sizes 6, 8, 10, 12, and 14.

FABRIC FINDER
Soft plaid cotton makes a perennial favorite choice for a boyfriend shirt. It is easy to handle, so the pattern can be cut on the bias for design detail. This basic shirt design can also be made up in pretty prints for a more feminine look.
Try these alternatives:
Brushed plaid cotton—Chambray—Denim—Gabardine—Linen—
Printed cotton—Printed cotton lawn

Materials
2¾ yd (2.5 m) of a plaid
   cotton, 54" (137 cm) wide
Ten buttons, ½" (12 mm) in
   diameter
Matching sewing thread
Contrasting topstitching
   thread

SKILLS SET
Working even slipstitch—**page 208** • Slipstitching double-fold hems—**page 210**
Stitching straight seams—**page 211** • Clipping curved seams—**page 212**
Finishing seams—**pages 214 and 215** • Easing—**page 223**
Making and applying bias binding—**pages 230 and 231** • Making buttonholes—**page 232**
Adding buttonholes—**page 233**

Pattern pieces

ENLARGE BY 500%

SIZE 6
SIZE 8
SIZE 10
SIZE 12
SIZE 14

EACH SMALL GRAPH
SQUARE = ³⁄₈" (1 CM)

FRONTS
Cut 2

BACK
Cut 1 on fold

COLLAR
Cut 2 on fold

POCKET
Cut 1

SLEEVE TABS
Cut 4

SLEEVES
Cut 2

FRONT YOKES
Cut 2

BACK YOKE
Cut 1 on fold

Cutting diagram

front
back
collar
collar
tab
sleeve
pocket
front yoke
back yoke

Cutting guide

Press the fabric thoroughly before cutting.

FROM THE FABRIC:

✂ Cut one shirt back, one back yoke, and two collar pieces, all on the fold.

✂ Cut two shirt fronts, two shirt sleeves, two front yoke pieces, four sleeve tab pieces, and one pocket piece.

A ⅜" (1 cm) seam allowance is included on all the pattern pieces, and a 1¼" (3 cm) hem allowance on the fronts, back, and sleeves. If you want a slightly longer or shorter shirt or sleeves, take this into account when cutting these pieces.

To make the shirt

1 STITCH ON THE YOKE

Press a ⅜" (1 cm) hem to the wrong sides at the straight bottom edge of all three yoke pieces. Lay the shirt back right side up and lay the back yoke right side up on top of it, aligning the neck and armhole edges. Baste in position. Topstitch along the folded edge of the yoke, ⅛" (3 mm) from the fold. Stitch the front yokes to the shirt fronts in the same way. Remove the basting.

2 STITCH THE SHOULDER SEAMS

With right sides of the back and fronts together and the raw edges aligned, stitch the shoulder seams, taking a ⅜" (1 cm) seam allowance. Press the seams open and finish the raw seam edges with zigzag or overlocking stitches if desired.

3 ADD THE FRONT BANDS

Cut a bias strip 3" (8 cm) wide and 1¾ yd (1.5 m) long, piecing strips together as necessary to obtain this length. Fold the strip in half lengthwise with right sides together and press. Open up the fold and press ¾" (2 cm) to the wrong side along both long edges. Fold the strip in half along the center again to form the bias binding. Using half of this bias binding for a band along each center front edge, bind each front edge with bias binding. Baste, then topstitch them in place. Remove the basting.

Try this...

If you're worried about working buttonholes neatly, use jeans-style snaps instead, which are no sew and come with a special punch tool.

4 PREPARE THE POCKET

Press ⅝" (1.5 cm) to the wrong side along all sides except the top edge. Baste these hems in place and topstitch ¼" (6 mm) from the fold. Remove the basting. Then press ⅝" (1.5 cm) to the wrong side twice along the top edge to form a double hem. Topstitch ⅜" (1 cm) from the top edge of the pocket.

5 STITCH ON THE POCKET
Position the pocket on the left front 2" (5 cm) below the yoke and 1¾" (4.5 cm) from the front band. Using a zipper foot, topstitch as close to the edge as you can around the sides and bottom edges.

6 PREPARE THE COLLAR
With right sides together, pin the collar pieces together. Stitch, taking a ⅜" (1 cm) seam allowance and leaving the neck edge open. Clip the corners, then trim the seam and press it open. Turn the collar right side out and press, positioning the seamline exactly on the fold.

7 STITCH THE COLLAR TO THE SHIRT
With raw edges aligned, pin the collar to the right side of the shirt, matching the ends of the collar with the edge of the front bands. Baste the facing layer to the shirt neckline. Stitch, taking a ⅜" (1 cm) seam allowance. Trim the seam and clip the curves. Press open. Turn and press the seam allowance of the collar to the inside. Pin it over the line of stitches along the inside of the neck. Using a zipper foot, topstitch as close to the edge as you can. Press. Lastly, topstitch along the outside edge of the collar, ¼" (6 mm) from the edge.

8 PREPARE THE SLEEVES
Place two sleeve tabs right sides together, matching the end points. Taking a ⅜" (1 cm) seam allowance, stitch along the long edges and the pointed end, leaving the straight end open. Clip the corners, trim the seams, press and turn right side out. Press again. Turn in the open end and slipstitch to close. Topstitch all around the tab ⅛" (3 mm) from the edge. Machine stitch a buttonhole at the pointed end of the tab, using topstitching thread. Position the straight end of the tab on the wrong side of the sleeve, about 13½" (34 cm) below the top of the sleeve. Stitch in position by sewing a square at the end of the tab and then a cross for security. In the same way, prepare the tab for the other sleeve and stitch it in position. Run easing stitches along the top of both sleeves.

9 STITCH ON THE SLEEVES

With right sides together, pin the sleeve to the armhole, matching the markers to the shoulder seam. Pull up the easing threads and even out the gathers. Stitch, taking a ⅜" (1 cm) seam allowance. Repeat with the other sleeve. Trim the seams and clip the curves. Press the seams open and then toward the sleeve. Finish the seam edges.

10 STITCH THE SIDE SEAMS

With right sides together, stitch the side seams, taking a ⅜" (1 cm) seam allowance. To do this, start at the hem, work up the side of the shirt to the armhole, and then carry on to stitch down the length of the sleeve. Trim the seams, press them open and then toward the back of the shirt. Finish the raw seam edges. Finally, topstitch along the full length of the seam through all layers, stitching ¼" (6 mm) from the seamline and catching in the seam allowance on the wrong side.

11 HEM THE SHIRT AND SLEEVES

Press ⅝" (1.5 cm) to the wrong side twice along the end of one sleeve to form a double hem. Topstitch close to the first fold. Repeat on the other sleeve and at the bottom edge of the shirt. Press.

12 MAKE THE BUTTONHOLES

Mark the positions for eight buttonholes on the right front—the first buttonhole is horizontal and is positioned at the end of the collar, the remaining seven buttonholes are vertical and are centered on the right front band. Machine stitch these buttonholes, using topstitching thread. Stitch buttons in position on the left front band. Stitch one button to the right side of each sleeve over the square of stitching joining the tab to the sleeve on the inside. Fold up the sleeve and button the end of the tab onto the sleeve button.

PATCHWORK THROW

This stunning patchwork throw is probably the easiest project in the book. It's just a matter of stitching the strips of upholstery fabric together and backing them with a lining fabric.

DIFFICULTY RATING: ⊞ ⊞ ⊞ ⊞ ⊞

This simple patchwork throw is made up of large strips that are quick and easy to piece together, designed to give you a taster of what may become an absorbing hobby. A centuries-old skill, the most beautiful and intricate patchworks are made up of tiny pieces (traditionally the good bits cut from worn clothes) exactingly pieced together to particular designs. This throw incorporates the general patchwork principles, but is made up of large pieces to create a throw for an armchair or sofa, or even a bed dressing. You can use the principles to make a throw any size simply by using more strips and cutting them longer.

THROW SIZE

The finished throw measures approximately 46½" x 63" (118 cm x 160 cm). For a bigger throw, see Cutting Guide on page 156.

FABRIC FINDER

This throw is made up of sumptuous, tactile furnishing fabrics in silk, velvets, and velour, but following craft traditions you can make the patchwork top in any fabric you like. The key is to choose fabrics that are all the same weight.
Try these alternatives:
Cotton shirting—Synthetic velvets—Printed cotton—Satins and sateens—Soft washed cotton—Silk—Washed silk

Materials

- ⅔ yd (60 cm) each of two different upholstery-weight fabrics (fabrics A and B), both at least 48" (122 cm) wide
- ½ yd (50 cm) each of two more upholstery-weight fabrics (fabrics C and D), both at least 48" (122 cm) wide
- 2 yd (1.7 m) of a solid-colored curtain-lining fabric, same width as strip fabrics
- Sewing thread in a neutral shade that works well with all the fabrics

SKILLS SET
Working even slipstitch—**page 208** • Stitching straight seams—**page 211**

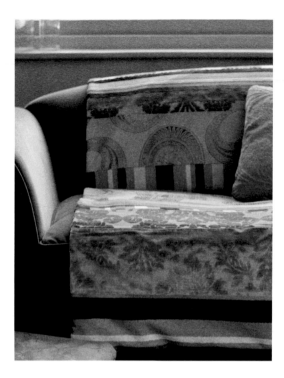

Cutting guide

For this throw, the 12 strips of varying depths were cut from fabric 48" (122 cm) wide, which determines the finished width. You can make a wider throw by using fabrics 60" (150 cm) wide. Alternatively, piece together two or more strips to make up any preferred width—cut the strips so that the joins don't all fall in the same place.

FROM FABRIC A:

✂ Cut three strips from selvage to selvage—one 3¾" (9.5 cm) wide, one 7½" (18.5 cm) wide, and one 9¾" (24.5 cm) wide.

FROM FABRIC B:

✂ Cut three strips from selvage to selvage—one 6¼" (16 cm) wide, one 8" (20 cm) wide, and one 9½" (24 cm) wide.

FROM FABRIC C:

✂ Cut three strips from selvage to selvage—one 3½" (9 cm) wide, one 5" (12.5 cm) wide, and one 8¼" (20.5 cm) wide.

FROM FABRIC D:

✂ Cut three strips from selvage to selvage—one 3¾" (9.5 cm) wide, one 4¾" (12 cm) wide, and one 8" (20 cm) wide.

A ⅝" (1.5 cm) seam allowance is included on all the fabric strips.

To make the patchwork throw

1 CUT THE STRIPS

Using the cutting guide, cut a total of 12 strips, from selvage to selvage. To match the featured throw, follow the given widths.

2 STITCH THE STRIPS TOGETHER IN PAIRS

Work out the best composition by laying out the strips right side up, side by side and with the long edges touching, rearranging them until you are happy with the look. With right sides together, pin the strips together in pairs along the long edges. Stitch together the first pair of strips. Repeat with all the other strips, so you end up with six pairs. Press the seams open.

3 STITCH THE PAIRS OF STRIPS TOGETHER
Now stitch the pairs together as precisely as possible, so you have three sets of four strips. Press the seams open as you work for perfectly flat pieces.

4 STITCH THE SETS OF STRIPS TOGETHER
Next stitch the three sets of strips together. Press the remaining seams open. Now press the wrong side of the patchwork top, using a hot iron and lots of steam and ironing parallel with the seams. Repeat on the right side. For fabrics with a deep pile, don't apply pressure behind the iron as this will flatten the pile. Instead, hover the iron over the fabric and use shots of steam. To neaten the outer raw edges, mark a line close to the edge of each side at right angles to the seam lines using tailor's chalk and a steel ruler. Use sharp dressmaker's shears to trim down this line.

5 COMPLETE THE THROW TOP
Lay the lining right side up on a flat surface and lay the patchwork top right side down on top of it. Smooth out the layers and pin them together around the outer edge of the top. Trim the lining to the same size as the patchwork. Stitch the top to the lining around the edge, leaving a 12" (30 cm) opening in the seam along one of the short sides. Press the seams flat to embed the stitches and also press the seam allowance back around the 12" (30 cm) opening. Clip off the corners of the seam allowances, taking care not to cut too close to the stitching.

6 HAND SEW THE OPENING
Turn the throw right side out through the opening. Then use a knitting needle (as it has a blunt point) to ease out the corners. Hand stitch the opening using even slipstitch to close it. Finally, press the whole throw flat so the seam lies exactly on the edge for a professional finish.

ROMAN SHADE

Smart and architectural, Roman shades are a classic window covering. They use a fraction of the fabric needed for curtains, so can be cost-effective. Take your time to work out the mathematical calculations.

DIFFICULTY RATING: ⊞ ⊞ ⊞ ⊞ ⊞

Materials

Shade fabric in the required amount

Lining fabric in the required amount

Matching sewing thread

Hook-and-loop tape, ¾" (2 cm) wide and as long as width of finished shade

½" (12 mm) plastic shade-rings, three per dowel

Metal cleat, to wrap cords around when shade is up

1" (2.5 cm) D-lath, ½" (1 cm) shorter than width of finished shade

⅜" (9 mm) round wooden dowels, each same length as lath and one for about every 12" (30 cm) of shade

1" x 1" (2.5 cm x 2.5 cm) support slat, ¼" (5 mm) shorter than width of finished shade

Staple gun

Four metal screw eyes

Three nylon shade cords, each twice length of finished shade plus width of shade

Shade pull

Being able to make your own Roman shade gives you endless fabric choices and can save you a small fortune. They've been given a three button rating because you need something of a mathematician's head to work out the positions of the dowel channels, but once you have, making the shade requires nothing more than stitching in a straight line. The extra skills that are essential, however, are meticulous measuring and a steady hand on the scissors.

ROMAN SHADE SIZE
The finished Roman shade can be up to 47" (120 cm) wide and the desired length. (If you want a wider shade, use more cords and make the shade in a similar fashion.)

FABRIC FINDER
Almost any furnishing or upholstery fabric will work for shades designed to cut out light. There's no reason why you shouldn't make a sheer version in crisp organdy, for example. However, as you'd be able to see through the shade to the cords, you may want to substitute organza ribbons for operating the shade.
Try these alternatives:
Cottons—Cotton mixes—Linen—Linen union—Furnishing synthetics

SKILLS SET
Working even slipstitch—**page 208**
Stitching straight seams—**page 211**

Measuring guide

FOR THE FINISHED SHADE WIDTH:

Decide whether you want the shade to fit inside the window recess or across it and measure this width—this is the finished shade width.

FOR THE FINISHED SHADE LENGTH:

Decide the position of wooden support slat at top of window, then measure from the top of the slat to where the bottom of shade should reach—this is the finished shade length.

Cutting guide

FROM THE SHADE FABRIC:

✂ Cut a panel of fabric that is as wide as the desired finished shade width plus 3" (8 cm) extra, and as long as the desired finished shade length plus 5" (13 cm) extra.

FROM THE LINING FABRIC:

✂ Cut a panel of fabric that is ½" (1 cm) narrower than the shade fabric panel. The length of the lining panel is the finished shade length, plus 1½" (4 cm) extra for each horizontal dowel channel. (This means that once the channels are folded and stitched, the lining is the exact length of the finished shade.) You will need one dowel channel every 12" (30 cm), starting from the top of the shade; below the last dowel channel there should be 6" (15 cm) to the bottom edge of the shade. The distance between the channels can be a little more, or less, but make the distance to the hem below the last channel, half of the distance between the dowels. To calculate how many dowel channels you need, draw the finished shade measurements to scale on graph paper and then draw lines across it at the position of each dowel—make sure the dowel channels are equally spaced.

To make the shade

1 CUT OUT THE SHADE AND LINING PANELS
Follow the measuring and cutting guides, cut out the shade and lining panels. Be sure to make a graph-paper scale drawing of the dowel positions on your shade as suggested—and keep it safe.

2 MARK THE DOWEL-CHANNEL POSITIONS
First, prepare the lining. Press 1½" (4 cm) to the wrong side along each side edge of the lining panel and baste in place. Now mark the dowel-channel positions across the right side of the lining. This must be done accurately so take your time. Referring to your scale drawing and using a retractable pencil, draw the first horizontal line the distance from the top of the lining as the first marked channel position. Draw a line 1½" (4 cm) below this—this is the first channel. Draw the remaining channel positions in exactly the same way—with two lines 1½" (4 cm) apart.

3 MACHINE STITCH THE DOWEL CHANNELS

With wrong sides together, fold the lining along the center of the first dowel channel, so the two marked lines are aligned, press well along this fold and then pin. Stitch ¾" (2 cm) from the pressed fold (along the marked line). Stitch the remaining channels in the same way.

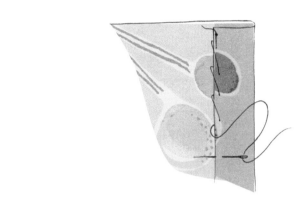

4 PREPARE THE SHADE FABRIC

Press 1½" (4 cm) to the wrong side along each side edge of the shade panel and pin in place. Then sew these hems in place along the raw edge, using a catch stitch that will be almost invisible on the right side of the shade. Next, at the bottom of the shade fabric, press ½" (1 cm), then 1½" (4 cm) to the wrong side. At the top of the shade fabric, press 1½" (4 cm) to the wrong side twice. These pressed folds now indicate the positions for the top and bottom hems—do not pin or baste these hems yet. Now unfold the second fold of the double hem at the top of the shade, so only the first 1½" (4 cm) is folded to the wrong side. Pin the soft section of the hook-and-loop tape to the right side of the shade fabric, just above the second pressed foldline so it sits on the double layer of fabric. Stitch the hook-and-loop tape in place all around its edge.

5 SLIPSTITCH THE LINING TO THE SHADE PANEL

With the top and bottom shade hems unfolded and with wrong sides together, lay the lining fabric on top of the shade fabric. Position the lining so its top edge is aligned with the hemline fold at the top and the bottom edge is aligned with the hemline fold at the bottom. Then center the lining widthwise on the shade fabric, so there is ¼" (5 mm) more shade fabric along each side edge. Pin and slipstitch the sides of the lining to the shade fabric between the dowel channels.

6 SLIPSTITCH THE TOP AND BOTTOM HEMS

Fold the pressed hems at the top and bottom of the shade over the lining and pin. Slipstitch the top and bottom hems in place. At the top of the shade, slipstitch the sides of the hem together. Leave the sides of the hem at the bottom open, for inserting the lath.

7 SEW ON THE RINGS

Measure and, using a pencil, mark three ring positions on each dowel channel. The cords will be threaded through these rings to pull up the shade. Mark one ring position in the exact center of the channel and one 1¾" (4.5 cm) from each end. Hand sew a ring at each of these positions, catching in the pressed channel fold.

8 INSERT THE DOWELS AND THE LATH

Slip one dowel into each channel and slipstitch the ends to close. Slide the D-lath into the hem channel at the bottom of the shade and slipstitch the ends to close.

9 PREPARE THE SUPPORT SLAT

Staple the hook section of the hook-and-loop tape to the front of the support slat. Screw the three screw eyes to the bottom of the slat, one 2" (5 cm) from each end and one at the center. Add an extra screw eye 1" (2.5 cm) from the pull-cord end. Fix a cleat to the window frame on the same side. Fix the support slat to the window.

10 THREAD ON THE SHADE CORDS

Knot one end of each cord onto one of the three rings at the bottom of the shade. Feed each cord up through the other rings to the top of the shade. Stick the shade to the support slat and then thread the cords through the screw eyes on the slat and out at the pull-cord side. With the shade down, align the cords and attach the shade pull to the ends, trimming the cords to the same length. Pull up the shade with the joined cord and secure on the cleat.

Try this...

To dress up the shade support slat, paint it the color of the shade or cover it by stapling a lightweight fabric over it.

BASIC DRESS

This simple dress is amazingly versatile. Made here in a lightweight plaid, it has a classic look and can be worn in the winter as a tunic over a blouse. Make it in black velvet and you have a Little Black Dress for the evening or try it in cotton for everyday wear.

DIFFICULTY RATING:

f you only want to learn to make one dress, then this is the one. It's an LBD—Little Basic Dress. It could be black, of course, but then it needn't be. You can choose the color, the print, and the fiber content without being limited by what happens to be in the shops this season. The reason this is the most useful dress to learn to sew is that it is almost a dressmaking sampler, incorporating most of the basic skills: darts, facings, and a zipper. Best of all, it doesn't use much fabric and it doesn't take long to sew.

DRESS SIZES
To fit women's sizes 6, 8, 10, 12, and 14.

FABRIC FINDER
This dress is made up in lightweight mixed-fiber plaid for an all season garment. Worn with a shirt and/or cardigan, it would also make a fun summer dress on its own. As a basic dress, however, most dress fabrics would work.
Try these alternatives:
Printed cotton—Linen—Cotton mixes—Linen mixes—Denim—Chambray—Velvet—Velour—Devore—Jacquard—Lightweight wool and wool blends—Mixed-fiber crepe—Shantung

Materials
1¾ yd (1.6 m) of a soft lightweight dress fabric, 54" (137 cm) wide
Matching invisible zipper, 17" (43 cm) long
Matching sewing thread

SKILLS SET
Working even slipstitch—**page 208** • Stitching straight seams—**page 211**
Slipstitching double-fold hems—**page 210** • Clipping curved seams—**page 212**
Finishing seams—**pages 214 and 215** • Stitching darts—**pages 220 and 221**
Inserting an invisible zipper—**pages 228 and 229**

165

ENLARGE
BY 500%

Pattern pieces

FRONT-NECK/
ARMHOLE FACING
Cut I on fold

BACK-NECK/
ARMHOLE FACING
Cut 2

FRONT
Cut I on fold

BACK
Cut 2

SIZE 6
SIZE 8
SIZE IO
SIZE I2
SIZE I4

EACH SMALL GRAPH
SQUARE = ³⁄₈" (I CM)

166

Cutting diagram

Cutting guide

Press the fabric thoroughly before cutting.

FROM THE FABRIC:

✎ Cut one dress front and one front-neck/armhole facing, both on the fold.

✎ Cut two dress backs and two back-neck/armhole facings.

A ⅜" (1 cm) seam allowance is included on all the pattern pieces, and 1¼" (3 cm) hem allowance on the front and backs.

To make the dress

1 STITCH THE DARTS
Mark and stitch the darts on the dress front and both back pieces. Press the waist darts toward the center of the dress and the bust darts downward.

2 INSERT THE ZIPPER
Insert an invisible zipper between the two back pieces and stitch the lower part of the seam, taking a ⅜" (1 cm) seam allowance. Press the seam open. Finish the raw edges of the seam with zigzag or overlocking stitches.

3 STITCH THE BACK AND FRONT TOGETHER
With the right sides of the back and front together, stitch the side seams, taking ⅜" (1 cm) seam allowances. Press the seams open. Finish the raw edges of the seam with zigzag or overlocking stitches. Leave the shoulder seams unstitched.

4 PREPARE THE FACING

With right sides together, pin, stitch the side seams of the all-in-one neck/armhole facing. Press the seams open. Finish the bottom raw edge of the facing with zigzag or overlocking stitches. As on the dress, leave the shoulder seams unstitched.

5 STITCH ON THE FACING

With right sides together, pin the facing to the dress, matching the side seams and aligning the neck and armhole edges. Pin and baste around the neckline and the armholes. Stitch, taking ⅜" (1 cm) seam allowances. Remove the basting. Trim the seams and clip the curves. Press the seams open.

6 STITCH THE SHOULDER SEAMS

Turn the facing to the inside of the dress and press. With the right sides of the dress together, stitch the shoulder seams, stitching through both the dress and facing and using a ⅜" (1 cm) seam allowance. Press the seams open and slipstitch the seam allowances to the dress along the outer edges. Turn in the ends of the facing near the zipper and slipstitch to the zipper tape close to the zipper.

7 STITCH THE HEM

Press ¼" (5 mm) to the wrong side along the hemline, then press 1" (2.5 cm) to the wrong side to form a double-fold hem. Machine stitch the hem in place, stitching close to the first fold.

VEST

A simple vest is surprisingly easy and hugely satisfying to make because once the lining is attached and it is turned right side out, all the seams are enclosed for an incredibly professional finish.

DIFFICULTY RATING: ⊞ ⊞ ⊞ ⊞ ⊞

Materials

1 yd (90 cm) of a wool twill, at least 54″ (137 cm) wide, for main fabric

1 yd (90 cm) of a contrasting wool twill, at least 54″ (137 cm) wide, for lining fabric

Two button molds, for ¾″ (2 cm) covered buttons, or two ¾″ (2 cm) buttons

Matching sewing thread

This one is designed for a man, but any vest is made using the same basic method. Endlessly versatile, the vest is the ultimate layering garment, especially in a woman's wardrobe. It can be used to smarten up any combination or bring a touch of the casual. A fashion favorite for a surprisingly long time, the vest has an illustrious past dating back to the seventeenth century. Originally from Persia, one of Charles II's returning ambassadors introduced the vest to the English court and it soon became de rigueur for English nobility.

VEST SIZES
To fit men's sizes S, M, L, XL, and XXL.

FABRIC FINDER
This vest has been made and fully lined in two shades of fine wool twill, which is a perfect choice for a traditional man's vest. Men's vests are generally made from suitings, wools or brocades while women's can be made in almost any dress fabric or suiting.
Try these alternatives:
Heavyweight cotton—Heavyweight linen—Denim—Silk brocade—Silk-wool mixes—Gabardine—Twill

SKILLS SET
Working even slipstitch—**page 208** • Stitching straight seams—**page 211**
Clipping curved seams—**page 212** • Stitching single-point darts—**page 220**
Making buttonholes—**page 232** • Adding buttonholes—**page 233**

Pattern pieces

ENLARGE BY 500%

FRONTS
Cut 2

CENTER BACK
Cut 1 on fold

SIDE BACKS
Cut 2

SIZE S
SIZE M
SIZE L
SIZE XL
SIZE XXL

EACH SMALL GRAPH
SQUARE = ³⁄₈" (1 CM)

Cutting diagram

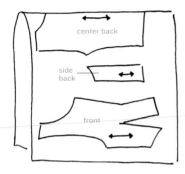

Cutting guide

Press the fabric thoroughly before cutting.

FROM THE MAIN FABRIC:

✄ Cut one center back on the fold.

✄ Cut two fronts and two side backs.

FROM THE LINING FABRIC:

✄ Cut one center back on the fold.

✄ Cut two fronts and two side backs.

A ⅝" (1.5 cm) seam allowance is included on all the pattern pieces. Be sure to draw around the front dart outline onto the wrong side of the main and lining front pieces with tailor's chalk, to ensure that you can stitch a precise dart shape.

To make the vest

1 STITCH THE DARTS
First, make the outer layer of the vest. Start by stitching the darts on the two main-fabric front pieces. Press the darts toward the center of the vest.

2 STITCH THE BACK PIECES TOGETHER
With right sides together, stitch the main-fabric back side panels to the main-fabric center-back piece. Trim the seams and press the seams open.

3 STITCH THE SHOULDER SEAMS
With right sides of the fronts and back together, stitch the shoulder seams. Trim the seams and press them open.

4 PREPARE THE LINING
Stitch the darts and all the seams on the lining pieces as for the main-fabric pieces.

Try this...

Making buttonholes through
two layers of wool isn't
easy. Even an experienced
seamstress would be advised
to practice making the
buttonholes on pieces of
scrap wool before attempting
it on the real thing.

5 STITCH ON THE LINING

Lay the outer main-fabric vest right side up on a flat surface and the lining right side down on top of it. Pin and baste along the back hemline; around the armholes; and then along the front hemline, up the front, around the neckline, and down the other front side and along its hemline. Stitch. Remove the basting. Trim the seams, clip the curves, and snip off the points, taking care not to cut into any of the stitches. Press the seams open.

6 STITCH THE MAIN-FABRIC SIDE SEAMS

Turn the whole garment right side out—first turn the back right side out through the open side seams, then pull the fronts right side out by pulling them through at the shoulders. Then with right sides together, stitch the side seams of the outer shell (through the open lining side seams). Press the seams open.

7 SLIPSTITCH THE LINING SIDE SEAMS

On the inside of the vest, at one side seam, fold the edge of the back lining piece over the front lining piece and pin. Slipstitch to close. Repeat with the other lining side seam.

8 COVER THE BUTTONS AND MAKE THE BUTTONHOLES

If you are using covered buttons, make two covered buttons, using the contrasting wool twill lining fabric. Mark positions for two horizontal buttonholes on the left front, about 3" (7.5 cm) apart and centered on the overlap. Machine stitch one buttonhole in each of the marked positions. Sew the buttons to the right front in corresponding positions.

TOTE BAG

A practical tote bag is a very useful accessory. Make yours a one-off original in canvas for the beach or in an upholstery fabric in an interesting print.

DIFFICULTY RATING: ⊞ ⊞ ⊞ ⊞ ⊞

Stitch up a smart tote bag to complement your wardrobe. Once you've got the knack, you can sew several more—either to suit the changing seasons or make as presents. This tote is designed with suede leather handle details for a super chic finish, though the idea can be easily adapted for cloth handles should you be daunted by the idea of stitching leather.

TOTE BAG SIZE
The finished bag measures 13" (33 cm) wide x 11" (28 cm) tall, and has a 3¾" (9.5 cm) wide gusset.

FABRIC FINDER
Tote bags need to be robust, hold their shape, and resist the dirt. For this reason, strong, tightly woven fabrics are the best—though be warned, stitching through several layers can be a challenge if you use too heavy a fabric. The lining can always be made in a lighter fabric. If you're daunted by machine stitching leather, make the straps in fabric, too.

Try these alternatives for the outer cover:
Any upholstery fabric—Cotton ducks—Light canvas—Denims—Cotton drill—Gabardine—Ticking

Try these alternative for the lining:
Lightweight printed cottons—Tana lawn—Dress lining (acetate)

Materials
- ½ yd (50 cm) of a medium-weight fabric print, at least 45" (115 cm) wide
- ½ yd (50 cm) of lining fabric, at least 45" (115 cm) wide
- 18" x 36" (50 cm x 90 cm) of medium-weight iron-on woven interfacing
- 8" x 32" (20 cm x 80 cm) of soft lightweight leather, for handles
- Sewing thread to match the bag and lining fabrics, and the strap leather
- Topstitching thread to match both the bag and lining fabrics
- Topstitching thread that contrasts with the strap leather
- Four metal bag-handle loops, with ⅝" (1.5 cm) wide detachable cross-bars
- Sewing-machine needle (size 14/90) and leather sewing-machine needle (size 16/100)

SKILLS SET
Working even slipstitch—**page 208** • Stitching straight seams—**page 211**
Stitching curved seams—**page 212**

Pattern pieces

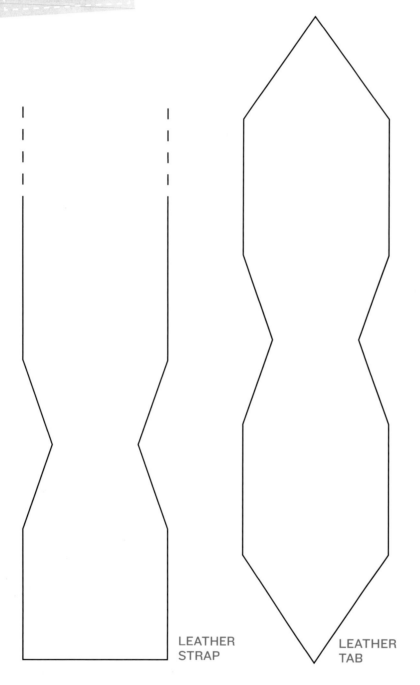

LEATHER
STRAP

LEATHER
TAB

Cutting guide

Press the fabrics thoroughly before cutting.

FROM THE MAIN BAG FABRIC:
✂ Cut one bag front and one bag back, each 14¼" wide x 12¼" (36 cm wide x 31 cm).
✂ Cut one bag gusset, measuring 5" x 35½" (12.5 cm x 90 cm).

FROM THE LINING FABRIC:
✂ Cut one bag back, front, and gusset the same size as the bag pieces.

FROM THE STRAP LEATHER:
✂ Cut two straps, each 1½" x 31¼" (4 cm x 79 cm).
✂ Cut four tab pieces, each 1½" x 7" (4 cm x 17 cm).

A ⅝" (1.5 cm) seam allowance is included on all the fabric pattern pieces.

To make the tote bag

1 SHAPE AND TOPSTITCH THE STRAP ENDS
Take one strap and, using the full-size template given for the leather strap, trace the shape onto the wrong side of the leather at one end. Trim along the outlines. Shape the other ends of the straps in the same way. Use a leather needle on the sewing machine and the contrasting topstitching thread on both the bobbin and upper thread, and set the machine to a long stitch length. Fold the strap end widthwise at the narrowest section and stitch together the two layers, stitching ⅛" (3 mm) from the edge on the two sides and ½" (1 cm) from the lower folded edge to allow the metal loop to pass through easily. Begin and end the stitching about ¼" (7 mm) past the two layers. On each strap end, make a small snip in the leather at each side of the fold—these snips allow the strap to fit neatly on the bag-handle loop.

2 TOPSTITCH ALONG THE LENGTH OF THE STRAP
Fold the long single-layer part of one strap in half lengthwise. Machine topstitch the length of the leather strap between the ends you have already prepared, ⅛" (3 mm) from the edge. Be sure to start and end the stitching so it overlaps the strap-end topstitching. Repeat for the other shoulder strap.

3 PREPARE THE LEATHER TABS
Take one leather-tab rectangle and, using the full-size template given for the leather tab, trace the shape on to the wrong side of the leather. Trim along the outlines. Shape the other leather tabs in the same way. Using ordinary thread that matches the leather, topstitch as for the strap ends, stitching ⅛" (3 mm) from the edge all around the tab except parallel to the fold where the stitching should be ½" (1 cm) from the fold to leave room for the bag-handle cross-bar. Make a little snip into the fold at each side as for the strap end. Prepare the remaining three tabs in the same way.

4 PREPARE THE MAIN BAG PIECES

Iron the interfacing onto the wrong side of the fabric print front and back. Next, trim the bottom corners of the front and back into gentle curves. (Remember that the top and bottom edges are longer than the bag is tall.) To do this, draw a lightly penciled gentle curve on the interfaced side on each of the two bottom corners, that is approximately ⅝" (1.5 cm) at its farthest from the corner point. Cut along the penciled lines.

5 STITCH ON THE LEATHER TABS

Place two leather tabs on the bag front, 4" (10 cm) down from the top and 2" (5 cm) in from each side. Use self-adhesive tape instead of pins to keep them in position. Using the contrasting topstitching thread, stitch around all sides following the first line of topstitching.

6 PREPARE THE LINING PIECES

So that the lining will sit more comfortably inside the bag, trim off ⅜" (1 cm) from the bottom edge of the front piece. Then trim a little off both side edges—start at the bottom edge, cutting ¼" (5 mm) from the edge and as you near the top edge taper the amount to ⅛" (3 mm). Round the bottom corners as for the outer bag. Trim the back piece in the same way so that the front and back are now the same size.

7 STITCH THE LINING PIECES TOGETHER

Using matching thread and an ordinary sewing-machine needle, stitch the lining gusset to the lining front—down one side, along the bottom, and up the other side. Now join the back to the gusset, stitching in the same direction for the front seam. Take your time at the corners, sewing and gently easing the gusset fabric around them. Leave a 6" (15 cm) opening in one of the seams for turning the bag right side out.

Try this…

If you can only find metal bag-handle loops that are bigger or smaller than the ones recommended, make the strap ends and tabs wider or narrower at the folds to accommodate the different size.

8 TOPSTITCH THE LINING SEAMS
Press the lining seam allowances toward the gusset. Then using a matching topstitching thread, topstitch ⅛" (3 mm) from each seamline on the gusset side of the seam. Take special care when topstitching around the rounded corners. Topstitching is not just decorative, it provides extra strength as well.

9 SEW THE BAG PIECES TOGETHER
Repeat steps 7 and 8 for the outer shell of the bag, but don't leave an opening in one gusset seam this time. Remember to stitch both gusset seams in the same direction and place the topstitching on the gusset side of the seamlines.

10 STITCH THE LINING TO THE BAG
With right sides together, place the lining inside the outer shell and align the upper raw edges and pin together. Stitch around the top twice for extra strength.

11 TURN THE BAG RIGHT SIDE OUT
Remove the pins and turn the bag right side out through the opening left in the lining seam. Press the seam allowances toward the lining. Slipstitch the opening in the lining seam closed.

12 TOPSTITCH THE TOP EDGE OF THE BAG
Fold the lining back into the bag and press so that the seam between the two is on the uppermost edge and no lining can be seen from the front. To stop the lining coming out, topstitch ⅛" (3 mm) from this top edge all the way around using matching topstitching threads for both fabrics—use a top thread that matches the outer bag fabric and a bobbin thread that matches the lining fabric.

13 ADD THE FINISHING TOUCHES
Fold the bag sides in like a paper bag, so the outer fabric sides are pinched together. Starting at the top edge, topstitch along the fold for about 4" (10 cm) through all layers of the bag. This makes the bag "sit" better for a smarter look. Finally, attach the straps using the detachable metal handle loops, ensuring that the handles lay flat and are not twisting.

Try this...

It's always a good idea to stitch the lining before the bag as that way you can get a bit of practice in where it matters least and be able to perfect the technique before sewing the important outer layer.

183

BLOUSE WITH COLLAR

Gracefully feminine, a simple blouse is the dressmaker's staple. Make it in delicate silk or chiffon, like this, or choose a more robust plain or printed cotton or linen for effortless elegance.

DIFFICULTY RATING: ⊞ ⊞ ⊞ ⊞ ⊞

Materials

1½ yd (1.4 m) of a silk crepe, 45" (115 cm) wide, OR 1⅛ yd (1 m) of a silk, 54" (137 cm) wide, for main fabric

¼ yd (25 cm) of a sheer silk print, for collar

¼ yd (25 cm) of a cream silk, for collar interlining

¾ yd (70 cm) of contrasting double-satin ribbon, ⅛" (3 mm) wide (optional)

Sewing threads to match main fabric, collar fabric, and ribbon

A beautifully stitched blouse is a wonderful addition to a woman's wardrobe. But let's be realistic: collars can be tricky, buttonholes too easily spoiled and set-in sleeves a veritable trap for novice stitchers. So here's the solution: the prettiest blouse with no fastenings, a delightful cheat's Peter Pan collar, and simple-to-stitch short sleeves. You won't need much fabric, so you can afford to splash out on special materials.

BLOUSE SIZES
To fit women's sizes 6, 8, 10, 12, and 14.

FABRIC FINDER
You can totally transform the look of this blouse by using a printed fabric instead of a plain for the main fabric—small-scale prints for a feminine look or large-scale prints for a bold statement. Choosing a matching or contrasting collar is up to you, but use the same weight for both fabrics.
Try these alternatives:
Flowing synthetic silk—Soft fine cottons—Plain lightweight cotton prints—Fine jersey—Lightweight linens

SKILLS SET
Slipstitching double-fold hems—**page 210** • Clipping curved seams—**page 212**
Stitching French seams—**page 216** • Making and applying bias binding—**pages 230 and 231**

ENLARGE BY 500%

Pattern pieces

SIZE 6
SIZE 8
SIZE 10
SIZE 12
SIZE 14

EACH SMALL GRAPH SQUARE = ³⁄₈" (1 CM)

FRONT
Cut 1 on fold

BACK
Cut 1 on fold

COLLAR
Cut 4

SLEEVES
Cut 2

Cutting diagram

MAIN FABRIC

front

sleeve

back

COLLAR FABRIC

collar

INTERLINING FABRIC

collar

Cutting guide

Press the fabric thoroughly before cutting.

FROM THE MAIN FABRIC:

✄ Cut one front and one back, both on the fold.

✄ Cut two sleeves.

✄ Cut one bias strip 1½" x 32"(4 cm x 80 cm).

FROM THE COLLAR FABRIC:

✄ Cut four collars.

FROM THE INTERLINING FABRIC:

✄ Cut two collars.

A ⅝" (1.5 cm) seam allowance is included on all the pattern pieces, a ¾" (2 cm) hem allowance on the front and back, and a 1¼" (3 cm) hem allowance on the sleeves. Note that two collar pieces face one way and two the other way.

To make the blouse

1 PREPARE THE COLLAR
Place two collar pieces right sides together and place one interlining collar piece on top of this. Baste around the outer curved edge, then stitch. Trim the seam and clip the curves. Remove the basting and press the seam open. Turn right side out and baste around the curved seam. Prepare the other side of the collar in the same way. Topstitch around the curves close to the edge. Finally, remove the basting and press.

2 BASTE THE COLLAR IN PLACE
Fold the blouse front in half and mark the center of the neckline with a pin. Place the collar pieces on the front, using the marker pin to center them and aligning them with the raw edges of the neckline and shoulder seams. Baste in position.

3 STITCH THE SHOULDER SEAMS
Using the French seam method, stitch the shoulder seams. To do this, first place the front piece on the back piece, with wrong sides together, and pin along both shoulders. Baste, then stitch each shoulder seam ¼" (5 mm) from the edge. Remove the basting and press the seams open. Now, fold along the seamline so the front and back are positioned with right sides together. Stitch again, but this time ⅜" (1 cm) from the fold.

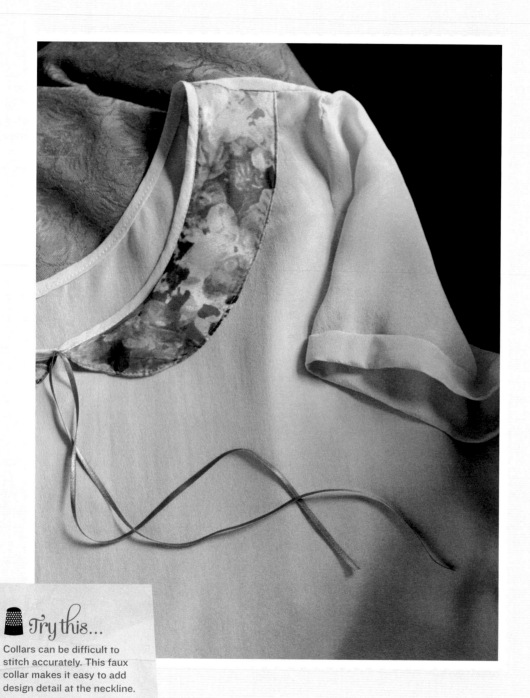

🪡 *Try this…*

Collars can be difficult to
stitch accurately. This faux
collar makes it easy to add
design detail at the neckline.

4 PREPARE THE SLEEVES

Turn under and press ¼" (5 mm), then ⅜" (1 cm) to the wrong side along the bottom of one sleeve to form a double hem. Baste, then stitch the hem. Fold the hemmed sleeve in half lengthwise and mark the center of the top of the sleeve with a pin. Repeat with the other sleeve.

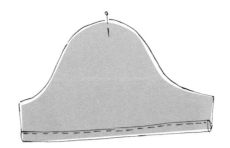

5 SEW ON THE SLEEVES

With wrong sides together, pin one sleeve to the body of the blouse, matching the marker pin with the shoulder seam. Stitch ¼" (5 mm) from the edge, then complete the French seam as for the shoulders. Repeat with the other sleeve.

6 STITCH THE SIDE SEAMS

Using the French seam method again, sew the side seams from the bottom edge of the blouse up to the sleeve seam and up the underarm seam—this means stitching the seam first with the wrong sides together (as shown) and then with the right sides together.

7 STITCH THE BLOUSE HEM

Turn up and machine stitch a double hem around the bottom edge of the blouse, folding up ⅜" (1 cm) twice to form the hem.

8 ROLL UP THE SLEEVE HEMS

Fold up ⅝" (1.5 cm) twice along the hem of one sleeve and press. Make discreet stitches at the armpit and at the outside center point to hold the fold-up in place. Do the same on the other sleeve.

9 BIND THE NECK EDGE

Starting at the right shoulder, pin and baste the bias binding strip to the neck edge with right sides together. (When you reach the starting point again at the right shoulder, sew the ends of the strip together.) Stitch the binding in place, using a ⅝" (1.5 cm) seam allowance. Remove the basting and trim the seam allowance to ¼" (6 mm). Fold under ¼" (6 mm) along the edge of the binding, then baste this fold to the wrong side just over the neck seamline. With the right side of the blouse facing you, topstitch along the neck binding close to the seamline—this will catch in the fold on the wrong side. Remove the basting and press. For a finishing detail, fold the narrow ribbon in half and stitch the fold to the center front neckline. Trim each length of ribbon to about 12" (30 cm) long, cutting on the diagonal, then tie in a bow.

BUTCHER'S APRON

This man's apron is so easy to make. You could easily knock one up in an afternoon and surprise the man in your life with a home-made present.

DIFFICULTY RATING: ⊞ ⊞ ⊞ ⊞ ⊞

Materials

- 1¼ yd (1 m) of a medium-weight striped fabric, 45″ (115 cm) wide, for apron and pocket
- ¾ yd (70 cm) of a lightweight denim fabric, 45″ (115 cm) wide, for bias binding
- Pair of metal D-loops to fit a 1″ (2.5 cm) wide neck strap
- Matching sewing thread

Back in the 1960s grade-school children often cut their sewing teeth on a simple apron. Granted, it was usually a rather more feminine affair than this one, but the principle of making something simple to wear also holds true for this smart but practical butcher's apron.

APRON SIZE
The finished man's apron is 34¾″ (88 cm) long from the top of the bib to the hemline.

FABRIC FINDER
Butcher's aprons need to protect against splashes and stains, so choose robust fabrics. Choose a lighter weight fabric to make the bias binding.
Try these alternatives for the apron:
Cotton duck—Denim—Medium-weight canvas—Gabardine—Cotton twill
Try these alternatives for the bias binding:
Chambray—Lightweight cotton

SKILLS SET
Working even slipstitch—**page 208** • Slipstitching double-fold hems—**page 210**
Making and applying bias binding—**pages 230 and 231**

Pattern pieces

EACH SMALL GRAPH SQUARE = ⅜" (I CM)

APRON
Cut I on fold

Try this...

Stitching through several layers of either medium-weight or heavyweight fabric, such as when attaching the apron pocket, is much easier when all the pieces are all basted securely in place before being machine stitched.

Cutting guide

Press the fabrics thoroughly before cutting.

FROM THE STRIPED FABRIC:

✂ Cut one apron piece, on the fold and with the stripes running vertically.

✂ Cut one pocket, measuring 11¾" x 10½" (30 cm x 27 cm), with the stripes running parallel to the longest edge.

FROM THE DENIM FABRIC:

✂ Cut enough 3½" (9 cm) wide strips on the bias to make a continuous bias binding at least 138" (350 cm) long.

To make the apron

1 PREPARE THE POCKET

On the pocket piece, turn ⅜" (1 cm) to the wrong side along the bottom edge (parallel to the stripes) and pin; then turn under ⅜" (1 cm) along the side edges as well. To miter the bottom corners to neaten them, fold back the corner at an angle, running between the outer corner and the inner corner where the hems meet. Unfold the pressed hems and the miter, then snip away the surplus fabric as shown. Refold the corner in position and press again. Baste these hems in place.

2 HEM THE POCKET

Turn under ¾" (2 cm) twice along the top of the pocket to form a double hem and pin. Baste the double hem in place and stitch it close to the first fold. Remove the basting along the pocket top but keep the basting in place along the sides and bottom edge. Press the prepared pocket and set it aside.

3 HEM THE APRON EDGES

Turn under ⅜" (1 cm) twice along the top of the apron bib. Stitch this double hem in place close to the first fold. Stitch a double hem along the sides and bottom of the apron in the same way, mitering the hemline corners. (Leave the armhole edges raw as these will be bound by the bias binding.) Press.

4 SEW ON THE POCKET

Position the pocket right side up on the front of the apron between the markers and baste. Topstitch the pocket to the apron along three sides, ⅛" (3 mm) from the edge. Remove the basting and press.

5 PREPARE THE BIAS BINDING

Stitch the 3½" (9 cm) wide bias-cut strips together end to end with ⅜" (1 cm) wide diagonal seams to produce a continuous strip of binding at least 138" (350 cm) long. Fold the strip in half lengthwise with the wrong sides together and press. Then open out the strip, fold ¾" (2 cm) toward the center along each long edge and press. Now refold it along the center and press again for a 1" (2.5 cm) folded binding width. Cut the strip into two lengths with squared ends—one 73½" (187 cm) long and one 56" (142 cm) long. Turn ⅜" (1 cm) to the inside along each short end of each of these binding pieces and pin these hems in place.

6 STITCH ON THE BINDING

With the apron right side up, pin the longest strip of prepared binding to the armhole on the right-hand side of the apron. To do this, leave 33½" (85 cm) of the binding free at the bottom of the armhole for the waist tie and then pin the binding evenly along the armhole with the apron sandwiched inside the binding—this leaves about 25½" (65 cm) free at the bib end for the neck strap. Pin the shorter binding strip to the other side of the apron in the same way, again leaving 33½" (85 cm) free for the waist tie—this leaves about 8" (20 cm) free at the bib end for the neck strap. Baste the entire length of each binding strip together along the folds, catching in the apron where the strips are pinned to the armhole. Topstitch the binding ⅛" (3 mm) from the edge, including along the waist tie, armhole, neck strap, and the turned under short ends. Remove the basting and press the binding.

7 SEW ON THE D-LOOPS

Thread a pair of metal D-loops onto the end of the longest neck strap, fold 2¾" (7 cm) of the strap to the wrong side, and slipstitch the last ¾" (2 cm) in place. Lace the short neck strap onto the D-loops ready to be adjusted.

Try this...

If you find making bias binding tedious, look for a bias binding maker. It's a small metal handtool that makes quick work of all the folding. It comes in many sizes, though a good standard-size bias binding is 2½" (6 cm) wide cut but not folded.

RUFFLE PILLOW

This pillow is modern yet fun, kept smart by teaming a neutral pleated grosgrain trim with the bold main color.

DIFFICULTY RATING:

P illows are great beginner projects. They don't demand too much fabric and are essentially just two squares or rectangles stitched together, yet they can be surprisingly expensive to buy.

By stitching your own, you can afford to use the very best fabrics and trimmings, to quickly, easily, and inexpensively bring a whole new look to your interior. If you're going to make your own pillows, it's always lovely to add your own creative touches with frills, trims, or piping. Most are stitched into the seams of the pillow, and the pleated ribbon on this one demonstrates the basic method. If you don't feel ready to put in a zipper, then slipstitch the cover to enclose the pillow form, and when it comes to laundering, just undo the slipstitching, wash, and re-slipstitch to close up again.

PILLOW SIZE
Excluding the ruffles, the finished pillow measures 19¾" x 11¾" (50 cm x 30 cm).

FABRIC FINDER
Scatter pillows can be made and trimmed with almost any fabric, including dress fabrics, though furnishing fabrics are more hard-wearing. A closely woven, medium-weight to heavyweight wool like this is great for pillows as it resists stains and doesn't crease.
Try these as alternatives:
Cotton—Silk—Linen—Brocade

Materials
½ yd (40 cm) of a medium-weight to heavyweight, closely woven fabric, at least 45" (115 cm) wide
1½ yd (1.4 m) of striped grosgrain ribbon, 1½" (4 cm) wide
Matching invisible zipper, 20" (50 cm) long
Matching sewing thread
Pillow form, 19¾" x 11¾" (50 cm x 30 cm), to fit finished cover

SKILLS SET
Stitching straight seams—**page 211** • Finishing seams—**pages 214 and 215**
Inserting an invisible zipper—**pages 228 and 229**

Cutting guide

Press the fabric thoroughly before cutting.

FROM THE FABRIC:

✀ Cut two pieces of fabric, each 20¾" x 12¾" (52 cm x 32 cm).

FROM THE GROSGRAIN RIBBON:

✀ Cut the length of ribbon into two equal lengths.

A ½" (1 cm) seam allowance is included on the fabric pieces.

2 **INSERT THE INVISIBLE ZIPPER**
Insert the invisible zipper along one long edge between the two pillow cover pieces, making sure it is centered with a 1¼" (3 cm) allowance at each end. Take a ½" (1 cm) seam allowance when inserting the zipper.

3 **STITCH THE COVER TOGETHER**
Open the zipper, then pin the two cover pieces with right sides together. With the piece with the ruffle stitching line facing upward and starting at one end of the zipper, stitch the two layers together, taking a ½" (1 cm) seam allowance and ending at the other end of the zipper. Stitch just outside the ruffle stitching so it won't show when you turn the cover right side out. Also, take care not to catch the side of the ruffle into the seam. Trim off a triangle of fabric at each of the corners. Turn the cover right side out, pushing out the corners using a knitting needle or any other blunt point. Press firmly. Insert the pillow form and zip up.

To make the ruffle pillow

1 **PLEAT AND ADD THE RUFFLES**
Take your time over this stage and aim for precise, even pleats. First, lay one pillow piece wrong side down on a flat surface. Turn under ½" (1 cm) twice along one short end of the grosgrain to make a double hem and, with right sides together, pin this end to one short edge of the pillow piece, placing it ⅝" (1.5 cm) from the end to allow room for the seam allowance. Make even pleats, pinning them to the edge of the fabric as you go and finishing ⅝" (1.5 cm) from the end. Viewed from the right side, each of these pleats should be 1³⁄₁₆" (3 cm) wide, and have a return of about ⅝" (1.5 cm). You should end up with ten pleats 1³⁄₁₆" (3 cm) apart. At the end of the ruffle turn under a ½" (1 cm) double hem again. Stitch the grosgrain to the fabric piece using a ½" (1 cm) seam allowance. Stitch the grosgrain to the other end of the pillow in the same way, ensuring the pleats lie in the same direction as they do on the other side of the pillow.

BASIC SEWING SKILLS

START SEWING

Sewing from scratch seems intimidating, but start with something simple and suddenly it all seems less daunting. The key is to choose a simple pattern that doesn't have too many difficult bits like collars, inset sleeves, and buttonholes. Each of our projects is designed for new (and newish) sewers, and some incorporate "cheats" to make the skills even more beginner-friendly. Take the time to build up your skills as you set out on your sewing journey. If there's anything you don't understand, refer to Basic Sewing Skills which is a fully illustrated guide to elementary sewing knowhow.

Start with your work station

Have a flat, clear surface for cutting out. In the absence of a large cutting table, this could be the floor. When sewing, position the sewing machine on a clear table so the fabric can lie flat and move freely as you sew.

Keep your work neat

Snip off trailing threads and badly frayed edges as you go. If you don't, they'll soon get jammed under the needle and snarl up the machine.

Basting knowhow

To begin with, pin and temporarily hand sew (baste) at every stage so you can make sure all the pieces are lying correctly before you machine stitch. As you become more experienced, you'll sometimes be able to go straight from pinning to machining. This will depend on what you're trying to do and the fabric you're working with. The project instructions don't tell you to baste every time because that will depend on your experience level. But there are times when you really should baste, such as setting in a sleeve or putting in a zipper, and at those times, the instructions include basting.

Handling fabric

One of the most important sewing lessons to learn is how to "ease" the fabric. When making garments, sometimes the cut pieces look as if they'll never fit together. Set-in sleeves are an example. The sleeve head is obviously larger than the armhole. By running easing stitches and pulling them up to fit the armhole, you're making the top of the sleeve curve over the shoulder. Sometimes, easing is more subtle and you need to pull one piece of fabric to fit the piece you're sewing it to. All this you will learn-by-doing and improve with experience.

Keep pressing

An ironing board and hot iron are key players in any sewing room. Experienced dressmakers can't stress enough how often you need to press your piece. This is because if all the seams are good and flat, the pieces will fit together better. Also, the steam in the iron helps to even out stitches and mold pieces into shape (such as round the curve of an armhole). The more steam you can use and the hotter the iron, the better. For safety, always test the heat on a spare piece of fabric. Not all fabrics can stand too much heat; the aim is to get the iron as hot as possible for that particular fabric.

✃ SEAMS
Generally seams need to be pressed open. Sometimes, both parts of the seam allowance need to be pressed in the same direction. The project instructions explain when this is needed.

✃ GATHERS
Gathers should be opened out, not flattened. Where gathers have been stitched into a band, lay the widest part of the fabric on the ironing board and hold up the gathered edge. Starting at the flat part of the fabric, iron in toward the gathers.

✃ CURVES
The aim is to retain the shape, not to flatten it. Put the curve over the end of the ironing board, choosing the pointed end or the squared end, depending on the size or shape of the curve. Alternatively, hold the piece up vertically and iron into the curve. Depending on the shape of the piece, you may have to "roll" it as you iron.

✃ KEEP IT CLEAN
Use a cleaning stick to keep the sole plate of the iron clear of residue.

ORDER OF WORK

Working in a logical order is key to a professional finish. Here's a "template" of good practice that can be adapted to suit individual projects.

1 LAUNDER THE FABRIC
Not all new fabrics are pre-shrunk, so launder your material following the care label before cutting out. Miss this step at your peril. You may put your heart and soul into making a garment, only to find it loses body, shrinks, or becomes misshapen the first time it's washed.

2 PRESS THE FABRIC
Press out any creases and folds using plenty of steam and the hottest iron setting possible that suits the fabric. Pull it back into shape if necessary. Trim any uneven edges.

3 PREPARE THE PAPER PATTERN PIECES
Cut out the pieces needed for the garment and iron them using a very cool iron. Adjust them if necessary.

4 CUT OUT THE FABRIC PATTERN PIECES
Follow the cutting layout provided for each of the garment projects. For most home furnishings, it's more a case of cutting squares and rectangles to size (see page 17).

5 TRANSFER THE MARKINGS
Ensure you transfer all the markings on the pattern pieces to all the fabric layers (see page 17).

6 STITCH THE DARTS
These are also easiest to handle while the piece is at its least complicated.

7 PUT IN THE ZIPPER
Put the zipper in at as early a stage as possible as that way, there will be less fabric to handle and the pieces will still be flat. Depending on the design (for example, if a dress zipper runs through separate bodice and skirt pieces), it might not be possible to make this the first step.

8 PIN, BASTE, STITCH, AND FINISH THE MAIN SEAMS
Beginners will want to go through all these steps at every stage. As you become more experienced, you may not want to baste every step. It is good to finish all the seams as you work (pages 214–215). If you have an overlocker you may prefer to finish the seams before stitching them.

9 STITCH ON FACINGS
Once the facings are stitched on, the garment is much more stable and easier to handle. Also, all the raw edges under them are protected from fraying.

10 STITCH THE BODICE TO THE SKIRT OR STITCH ON THE WAISTBAND
This is one of the final stages as, after this point, the garment becomes larger and more difficult to handle.

11 PREPARE AND INSERT SLEEVES
If the garment has a dropped sleeve that doesn't need easing, a loose shirt, for example, it can be easier to put the sleeve in before sewing the side seams. That way, you can stitch up the side seam and down the sleeve all in one.

12 FINISHING TOUCHES
Hems, buttons, buttonholes, hooks, eyes, and snaps are all added when the garment is all but finished.

Try this...

Aim to make your piece look every bit as good from the inside as the outside. This is not just for the glowing feeling of a job well done: it's because the neater the finish, the better the whole garment looks and hangs.

BASTING

Basting is making temporary hand stitches to hold pieces of fabric together before and during machine stitching. There are two purposes: first, to secure the pieces so that you can make sure they fit together well and lie flat before offering them to the machine; and second, to temporarily hold a garment together for fitting purposes. As you become a more experienced stitcher, you may not need to baste absolutely everything, depending on the fabric and complexity of the construction. Pins put in at right angles to the seamline (so that the machine can run over them) can suffice if you have a long, straight seam and you're using a stable fabric, such as cotton. However, even the professionals prefer to baste if they are working with a stretchy or slippery fabric. It's also good to baste anything that is difficult to stitch, such as putting in zippers or sleeves, or stitching around curves. If it feels laborious, cheer yourself with the thought that it's a whole lot better than ripping out uneven machine stitching. Choose a contrasting thread for basting—it's so much easier to see both while machining and removing it afterward.

EVEN BASTING

The most basic and usual form of basting that can be used in a variety of circumstances.

Using a contrasting thread, thread a needle with a single strand and knot the end. Bring the needle up from the underside, then make what's essentially a line of long, even running stitches.

Try this...

While you'll want to start off basting using thread that has been knotted at the end, it's not always necessary to secure the other end when you've finished, especially if you intend to machine the seam immediately. Then removing the basting once the seam has been stitched is just a matter of pulling the knotted end.

UNEVEN BASTING

This is a useful way to quickly baste long lengths, such as straight seams. It is similar to even basting, except the stitches are longer and the gaps shorter. For a more secure version, alternate long stitches with short stitches.

Bring the needle up from the wrong side, baste a long stitch, pass the needle back down to the wrong side, bring it up to the right side, baste a stitch no longer than the needle length, back down and up again in a single action. Now allow a long stitch again before repeating the down-up-down-up procedure again.

DIAGONAL BASTING

This is used to secure layers of fabrics over larger areas—for example, to stitch the body of a lining or interlining on drapes or lapels. Not designed to be seen, diagonal basting is always hidden in the structure of the garment or piece, keeping the fabric flat and stopping it from slithering about as you join the main pieces.

Baste parallel horizontal stitches at the back of the work to make long, even diagonal stitches at the front of the work.

Even if you're a dedicated machinist, there will be times when you need to finish off your work with hand stitches. The most useful and widely used are given here. None are difficult, but it takes practice before you'll automatically make stitches that are even both in length and tension.

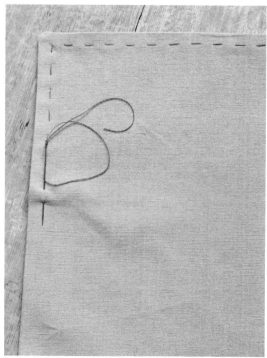

RUNNING STITCH

This is the simplest of stitches where you make a series of even stitches with even gaps. It is used as the basic stitch for hand gathering or easing.

Using a single strand of knotted thread, bring the needle through to the front from the underside of the fabric. Working from right to left (reverse this if you are left-handed), weave the needle in and out of the fabric, making both the stitches and the gaps between them the same length and taking several stitches onto the needle before drawing the thread through.

SADDLE STITCH

This is a smaller, neater version of running stitch. Sewn with the top, or right, side of the fabric facing upward, it can be used as a hand-sewn topstitch to define edges.

Make neat stitches about ⅛" (3 mm) long with even gaps.

206

Try this...

When hand stitching, cut the thread to about the same measurement as from your elbow to your fingertips. Longer than that and you'll get snarl-ups; shorter and you'll be forever having to re-thread the needle.

BACKSTITCH

Backstitch is the standard stitch that was generally used for seams in pre-sewing-machine days. It's still a good standby for small areas that are difficult to get to on the machine.

Using a single strand of knotted thread, bring the needle through to the front from the underside of the fabric. Make one running stitch. Now take the thread back to the end of the first running stitch, along the wrong side of the fabric and up again by the same length as the first stitch. Pull out any slack. Now go back to the point where the thread came out previously. As you work along the seam in this way, you will see that you have made what looks like a line of machine stitches. If you turn the fabric over to the wrong side, it won't look so neat as the stitches overlap each other. But the result is robust.

207

Try this...

If the two edges need a little easing, instead of holding them together as shown in the photograph, wrap them around your hand to take up a little slack where needed, then work the stitches.

EVEN SLIPSTITCH

This is one of the most useful finishing stitches to learn. It is used to join two folded edges—for example, where you are closing the opening in a seam in an item that has been turned through. The idea is that you hide as much of the stitch inside the foldlines of the fabric.

1. Pass the needle from the inside of the fold to the front, take a tiny stitch into the opposite fold, pass the needle along inside the fold and bring it out to the front, then take a tiny stitch into the first fold and pass the needle along that first fold.

2. When you get to the end, take two tiny stitches on top of each other in a concealed place to finish. The result is strong, secure, and neat.

UNEVEN SLIPSTITCH

Uneven slipstitch makes a neat job of joining a folded edge to a single main piece of fabric, as in a double-fold hem. It's worked in a similar way to even slipstitch, but you can only run the needle along the inside of the single fold, and you want to make as little impression on the front side of the main piece of fabric as possible.

1   When you bring the needle up from the inside of the fold, just take a couple of threads from the main fabric.

2   Next, bring the needle back to the fold and run it along the inside. Repeat along the length and finish with two tiny stitches on top of each other in a concealed place.

DOUBLE-FOLD HEM

A beautifully finished hem makes the difference to the overall look of a garment; but one that hangs perfectly evenly demands plenty of preparation. A double-fold hem is the dressmaking standard, encasing the raw edge and providing weight.

1 Turn the garment inside out and trim the ends of the seams that will lie within the hem to reduce bulk. Next, give all the seams a firm press. Once you have decided what length you want the garment to be, turn up and pin the hem near the fold. Check that it is lying straight, then baste close to the fold. Cut a length of cardboard for the hem to the desired depth of the hem. Use this as a template to mark off the hem, allowing an extra ⅜" (1 cm) for turning under, and trim off the excess. Press in ⅜" (1 cm) all along the raw edge, then pin the hem in place.

2 Now baste another line of stitches along the top fold. If you are making an A-line skirt, you might find there is excess fabric at the top fold to accommodate. If this is the case, run a short line of easing stitches to help spread the excess.

3 Use uneven slipstitch to work the hem. Bring the needle up from inside the fold, then pick up two or three threads from the main fabric. Run the needle along the inside of the fold again, then bring it out and take another tiny stitch in the main fabric. Continue to the end of the hem.

Purists would say that every seam should be pinned, basted, and then stitched, and we have included those steps in all our instructions. However, as you become more adept with the sewing machine, this won't always be necessary. For example, when stitching simple straight seams on nonstretchy, nonslippery fabric, many dressmakers dispense with the basting stage. Once you're confident enough to do this, you'll need to put the pins in across the seamline, rather than along it. That way, it's easy to remove the pins as you stitch, just before they reach the presser foot of your sewing machine. Curved seams, difficult-to-get-at corners or places where one piece of eased or gathered fabric is being stitched to a flat piece should be basted before being offered to the more hurried 'jaws' of the sewing machine. It's better to invest the time up front than risk a snarl-up that takes ages to unpick and might even damage the fabric in the process. It's also a good idea to baste slippery or stretchy fabrics before you stitch them.

STRAIGHT SEAMS

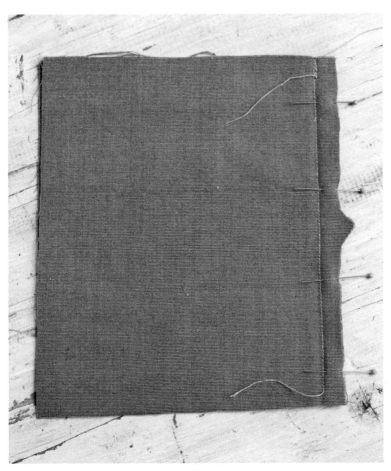

Place the two pieces of fabric right sides together, aligning the raw edges, and pin across the seams at intervals of about 6" (15 cm). Raise the presser foot. Place the fabric under the needle, ⅜" (1 cm) from the top edge, aligning the raw edges with the seam allowance marker guidelines that are etched onto the throat plate of your sewing machine. Press the reverse stitch switch and stitch backward to the top edge, then stitch forward from there all along the seam. At the end, stitch back up the seam by about ⅜" (1 cm) to finish. Press the seam open.

Try this...

To keep a straight line, don't be tempted to watch the needle as you stitch: instead, keep your eye on the edge of the fabric running along the seam allowance marker on the throat plate.

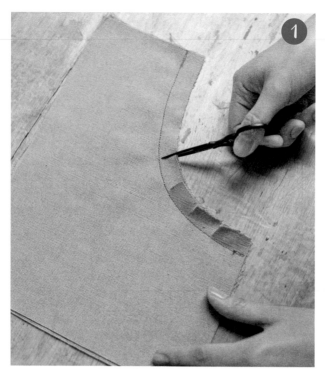

CURVED SEAMS

Sew curved seams in exactly the same way as you would a straight seam. The key is to keep your eye on the raw edge of the seam, making sure that it aligns with the seam allowance marker on the throat plate at all times. This will mean that you automatically turn the fabric smoothly with the curve to create an even seam allowance. Finally, press the seam open.

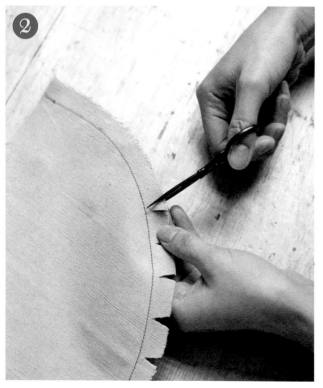

① CLIPPING INWARD CURVES
Seams that curve inward need to be trimmed close to the seam and clipped using the points of sharp scissors. This allows the edge to curve inward once the piece is turned right side out.

② NOTCHING OUTWARD CURVES
Outward curves should be notched, by carefully snipping out tiny triangles of fabric from the seam allowance, making sure you don't snip into the stitches. This stops the seam allowance form forming bulky gathers once the piece is turned right side out.

SEWING AROUND CORNERS

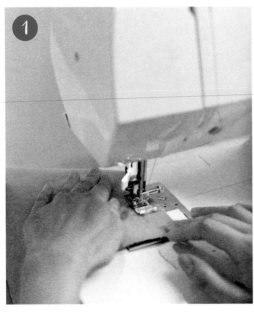

1 As well as seam allowance markers, most sewing machine needle plates have etched cross lines to help with accurate stitching around corners. If yours doesn't, stick masking tape across the throat plate in front of the needle at the standard seam allowance position of ⅝" (1.5 cm). Stitch down one side of the corner in the same way as you would a straight seam until the needle is level with the masking-tape marker. Leave the needle in the down position.

2 Lift the presser foot, swivel the fabric around until the new edge aligns with the etched seamline on the throat plate or with your own masking-tape marker.

3 Lower the presser foot and stitch down the new seam.

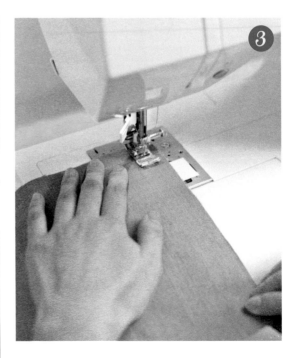

FINISHING SEAMS

Any seams that are not enclosed need to be finished to neaten them and stop the fabric from fraying. There are several ways to do this: which one will depend on the fabric, the capability of your machine, and speed.

PINKING

This is the quickest and simplest way to finish seams and a good solution unless you have a fabric that frays really readily, as the pinked edges would soon become eroded. Trim the seam allowance as close to the edge as possible. On finer fabrics, you can cut both layers at once. For thicker fabrics, press the seam open, then pink one side at a time.

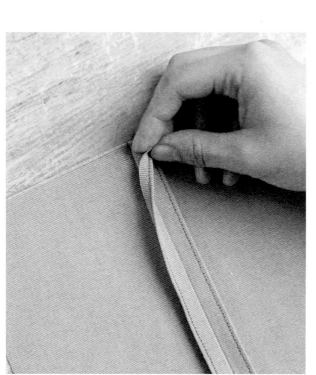

TURNING IN

Turn in and press ¼" (6 mm) to the wrong side. Set the machine to straight stitch and stitch. This is quick, easy and can be done on the same machine without changing the settings. Even an antique sewing machine could cope with this one.

214

1 Set the machine to a medium-width short zigzag stitch, then stitch down one seam allowance as close to the raw edge as possible. Make sure only the seam allowance is under the needle. When you've completed one side, turn the piece around so only the other seam allowance is under the needle.

2 Trim to neaten if you wish, taking care not to cut through any stitches. The finished seams are now both neat and flatter than turned-in finishing.

OVERLOCKING

This professional-looking finish can only be achieved using an overlocker, which is a separate and not inexpensive machine. It trims and finishes the seams in a single action and is sometimes even used to stitch the seams at the same time. However, as it cuts the fabric as it sews, amateurs can sometimes find they've cut into the main body of the garment at the same time, thereby ruining their work. If you do decide to invest in one, you can safeguard damaging your work by finishing the seams with the overlocker before, rather than after, sewing them.

215

Some garments need to be made using enclosed seams, where the raw edges of a first seam are enclosed within a second. These are usually used on items made of fine fabric worn close to the body, such as lingerie, or, at the other end of the scale, on hard-wearing workwear such as jeans.

FRENCH SEAMS

Lingerie, made from fine fabrics that are in constant contact with the skin, is usually made using French seams, which are strong, surprisingly hard-wearing, and look almost as good on the inside of the garment as on the outside.

1   With wrong sides together, pin and stitch the seam ¼" (5 mm) from the raw edge. Trim the seam to ⅛" (3 mm) and press open.

2   Turn the seam through so that the right sides are together, fold along the seamline, and press. Baste as close as you can to the first seam.

3   Machine stitch, stitching ⅜" (1 cm) in from the seamed edge, enclosing the raw edges, and reverse stitching at each end to secure. Press the seam to one side.

4   Finally, pull out the basting stitches. This will be easy unless the machined stitches encroach on the basting.

Try this...

Where possible, it is always a good idea to stitch your seams in the same direction to avoid puckering and help the seams to lie flat. This is because fabric moves slightly every time you stitch and if you stitch downward one time and upward the next, it will be pulling against itself.

FLAT FELL SEAMS

These are typically used on jeans. They are very robust, yet flat on the inside, so they don't rub the skin.

1 With wrong sides together, stitch a plain seam ⅝" (1.5 cm) from the raw edge, using a topstitching thread. Press the seam open and then press both seam allowances toward the back of the garment. Trim the underneath layer to ⅛" (3 mm).

2 On the untrimmed seam allowance, press ⅛" (3 mm) to the wrong side, then press this over the trimmed raw edge. Pin in position, placing the pins across the seam. Topstitch as close to the folded edge as possible.

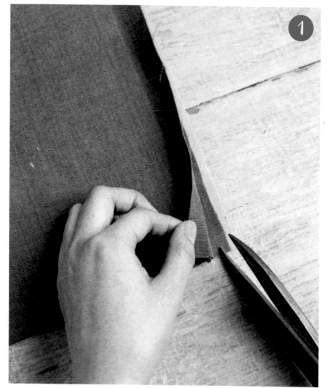

1 When a seam will not be visible because it is enclosed, for example on a collar, a facing, or a pillow cover, it must be trimmed. Otherwise the resulting seam will be bulky and won't lie flat. There are several ways to do this.

2

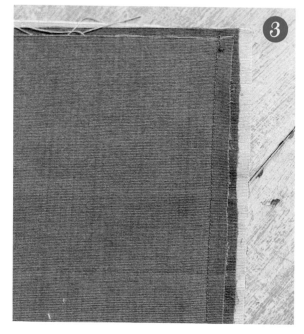

3

GRADING

It's especially important to reduce bulk when you are using heavy fabric, or where several layers are being joined (such as where the body of the garment and facings meet in several layers at the shoulder seams). To do this, you need to trim the seam allowances to different widths.

1 First, neaten the seams by trimming ¼" (6 mm) off all layers. Then, leaving the lowest layer, trim a little off the edge of the next layer.

2 Now trim a larger margin from the layer above that.

3 When all the layers have been trimmed to different margins, the seam allowance lies flatter.

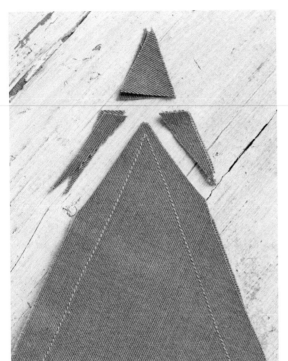

Always snip off corners before turning them right side out. Cut close to the stitches, but be careful not to snip into them. Where there is a particularly sharp point, start by cutting off the corner, then taper the sides to reduce the bulk. This will make for a neater point once it is turned right side out.

INTERNAL
CORNERS

To reduce bulk at internal corners, place a pin at the corner, just inside the line of stitching at the corner, then snip into it with sharp scissors. That way, you can be sure that you don't cut the stitches by mistake.

SHAPING AND CONTOURING

The art of dressmaking is transforming flat pieces of fabric into three-dimensional garments that fit the contours of the body. But even the simplest of garments relies on more than just joining straight seams. There are several ways to create shape: by using darts, gathers, and contoured seams.

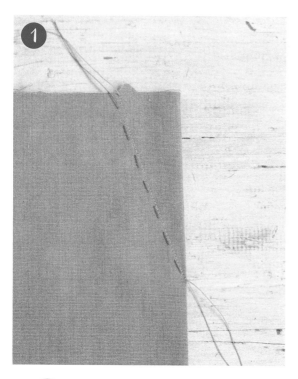

SINGLE-POINT DARTS

Plain or single-point darts are the most commonly used, predominantly to shape the waists of skirts and trousers. Whenever you sew a dart, always press the dart in the direction specified using lots of steam.

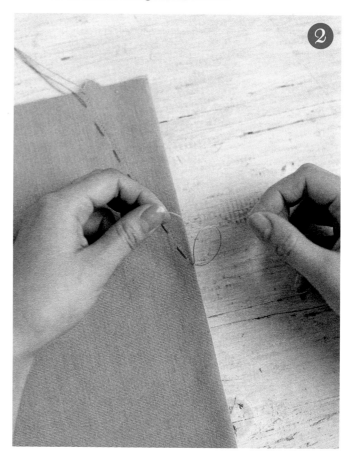

1 With right sides together, match the dots at the widest part of the dart to make a fold that reaches down to the single point at the end of the dart. Pin and hand baste just inside the stitching line. Machine stitch from the widest end of the dart to the point, then make two more stitches right on the fold to make a crisp, clean point.

2 To finish, tie the two ends of thread together in a knot at the tip of the dart and then remove the basting stitches.

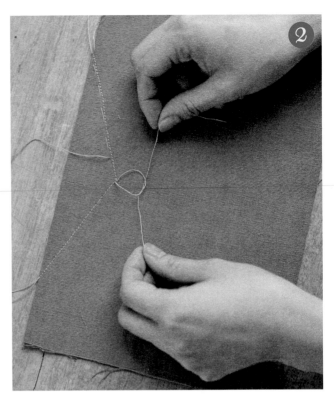

CONTOUR DARTS

Sometimes called double-point darts, contour darts are designed to nip in fabric on dresses—at waistlines, for example. Marked on the flat fabric, you're likely to have an elongated diamond shape with a point at each end, hence the name.

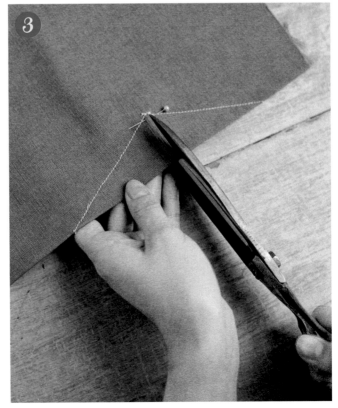

1. Match the markers right sides together at the widest points of the diamond shape and pin across the fold. In the same way, pin across the fold at intervals until you reach the single top marker. Repeat toward the bottom marker. Baste just inside the stitching line.

2. Starting at the widest point, stitch just inside the basting toward the top point of the dart. Return to the widest point again and stitch toward the bottom of the dart in the same way. Tie the pairs of threads together at the widest point and the points at each end.

3. The widest part will need to be clipped. Protect the stitches at the point by placing a pin just inside the stitching line before clipping with sharp scissors.

HAND GATHERING

Easy and fun, this is a simple first sewing skill to learn. As the gathering stitches are usually later enclosed into a waistband or otherwise hidden, there is less demand for perfection than with other skills, although it has to be said, the more even the gathering stitches, the easier it is to manage the next stage of stitching on the bodice or waistband and the better the end result.

1. Using contrasting thread, make a large knot in one end then sew a line of running stitches along the raw edge to be gathered. Ideally, the thread you're using should be at least as long as the edge to be gathered. This is not always possible. A full dirndl skirt, for example, may have such full gathers that the length of thread would be almost impossible to handle without getting tangled. In this case, divide off the length to be gathered into quarters and work four equal lengths of gathers.

2. When the line is complete, pull up the gathers to the desired length. Wind the spare pulled-up thread around a pin placed at the end of the line of gathers. That way, the gathers are stabilized while you even them out along the line. If, once you've pinned the gathered edge to the straight piece (waistband or bodice for example), you find you've not pulled it up enough, or too much, perhaps, you can unwind the spare thread from the pin, adjust, and re-wind.

222

GATHERING AND EASING

Gathering and easing both add fullness to the fabric, bringing three-dimensional shape to two-dimensional fabric without the need for darts.

EASING

Easing can be used where two pieces of fabric that are slightly different in length need to be joined. By easing, you can ensure that the ends align, as any slack can be taken up all along the length of the longer piece rather than bunched up at the end. Easing is also used to create shape at the top of a sleeve, for example. As the sleeve top is cut in a curve and is slightly larger than the armhole, when the easing is pulled up, it provides a 'shell' that curves over the natural curve of the shoulder. Easing lines are often made over only a part of the length of the seam and a commercial pattern will be marked with circles or dots to show where the easing should begin and end.

Run two lines of small running stitches between the markers. Place a pin at each end for easy adjustment, then pull up in the same way as gathering stitches (see opposite).

Try this...

Avoid the bunched up look on hemlines that widen toward the bottom, such as A-line skirts and flared trousers by running a line of easing gathers. That way, the excess fabric can be spread evenly over the whole hemline before stitching.

The most versatile of all fastenings, zippers are used not just in garments but also soft furnishings, such as loose sofa or chair covers. As well as being a practical way of getting in and out of garments, zippers have, in themselves, become a fashion statement. Sometimes zippers are invisible, hidden neatly away in the seam allowance, but they can also be "revealed" and as much a part of the project design as any trimming. The most usual insertion techniques are the centered zipper or the lapped zipper, often used for the fly on trousers. Putting in a zipper neatly takes practice and some methods are easier than others. The trick is to take your time and to pin and baste at every stage. You will need an ordinary zipper foot for most zippers, which comes as part of your machine's tool kit.

CENTERED ZIPPER

This is the traditional method of choice for center back zippers (on dresses for example) before the advent of invisible zippers. It is also the easiest to put in, and very versatile, so a good choice for beginners.

1   Start by using the zipper itself to measure the opening. Align the top of the tapes with the top raw edge of the garment, and place a pin on the garment seam allowance in the position of the zipper's end stop. Now, baste using contrasting thread, from this point down to the hemline, then machine stitch. Baste from the pin up toward the top raw edge of the garment. Press the seam open along its length.

2   Place the zipper face down on top of the seam allowance, with the teeth centered over the seamline and the raw edges of the tape meeting the top raw edges of the garment. Pin in position. Starting at the bottom, baste through all layers up one side to the top. Now baste through all layers on the other side, working in the same way from the bottom to the top. By working from the bottom to the top on both sides, rather than basting all around, the fabric will lie flatter. Turn the piece over to check that the basting is even on both sides of the zipper on the right sides.

224

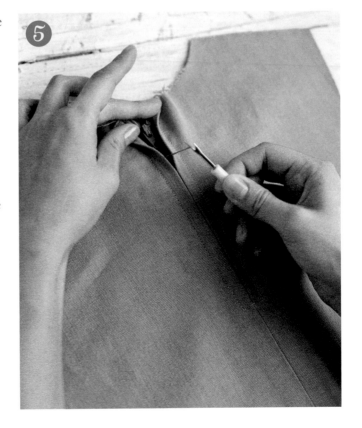

3 Fit a zipper foot, then place the piece with the bottom end of the zipper right sides up under the needle. Stitch up one side just outside the basting stitches. Finish by reverse stitching at the top, then re-position the piece with the needle at the bottom again. Stitch from the first line of stitches, across the bottom, then up the other side just outside the basting stitches. Reverse stitch to finish.

4 Now pull out the stitches basting the zipper in position. If you kept the stitching line just outside the basting, this will be easy.

5 Finally, remove the line of basting that temporarily joined the seam. Using a hand sewing needle, thread up the loose end at one side of the end of the zipper and pass through to the wrong side. Secure with several tiny stitches on top of each other. Repeat on the other side.

LAPPED ZIPPER

Traditionally used for side zippers in skirts and dresses, the lap should lie toward the back, giving a smooth line to the garment.

1. Start by using the zipper itself to measure the opening. Align the top of the tapes with the top raw edge of the garment, and place a pin in the garment seam allowance at the position of the teeth end stop. Pin, baste, and stitch down from this to the hemline. Press the whole seam open, including the unstitched part.

2. With right sides down, press open a ¼" (6 mm) more on the left-hand side.

3. Turn the piece over so the wrong sides are facing down. Fit a zipper foot on the machine. Close the zipper and position it under the pressed-back fold. Pin, baste, and stitch. When you get near the slider, leave the needle down, pull the slider to the part you've already stitched and stitch to the end.

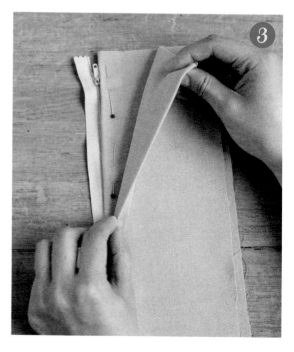

4 Lay the piece wrong sides down on a flat surface and pin the fold of the unstitched side of fabric over the stitched side. Using contrasting thread, baste along the bottom and up the unstitched side as far away from the teeth as possible, catching all layers.

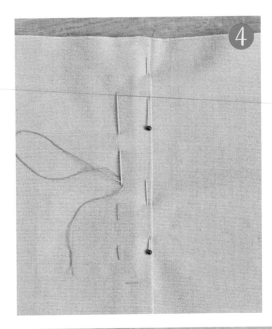

5 Now place masking tape over the basting stitches. This acts as a straight guide for stitching and also stops you from stitching over the basting stitches. Stitch across the bottom first, then up to the top. Peel off the masking tape.

6 For a neat finish, thread the loose machine thread at the end of the zipper onto a hand needle and pass the thread to the back. Use several small stitches on top of each other within the seam allowance at the wrong sides to secure.

227

INVISIBLE ZIPPER

For an invisible zipper, you need a special invisible zipper foot that allows you to stitch under the nylon coil. This doesn't come with most sewing machines so you will need to be buy it separately. An invisible zipper is not easy to put in, but with practice, you'll get the knack. Once it's hidden in the seamline, an invisible zipper gives a smart, tailored finish. While other zippers are stitched in from the bottom up, invisible zippers are stitched from the top down; for this reason, many people like to leave stitching the rest of the seam until after they have put in the zipper, rather than before.

1   Run a line of contrasting basting stitches along the seamlines of both pieces of fabric for the length of the zipper opening. Open the zipper and use a very cool iron to press the ridge of the coil over to the front sides of the tapes on both sides. Close the zipper and lay it face down over the basting on one side, aligning the top raw edges of the tapes with the top raw edges of the garment. Pin and baste in position.

2   Open the zipper. Starting at the top and with the coil under the right groove on the invisible zipper foot, stitch down the length of the zipper. Close the zipper. Align the top raw edges of the zipper tape with the top raw edges of the garment, pin, and baste the zipper over the line of basting on the other piece of fabric.

228

Try this...

Take your time with zippers and never cut corners on pinning and basting. The more accurately the zipper is put in, the easier you'll find neatly joining the next pieces. A well put in zipper makes a huge difference to the overall look of the whole garment.

3 Open the zipper again, then stitch it to the single layer of the other side, using the same method as you did the first side. Baste the lower part of the seam and stitch from the end of the zipper to the hemline. Finally, press the seam open and press the newly stitched-in invisible zipper.

4 Once the zipper has been inserted, use a good shot of steam to press the garment on the right side. This will neaten the zipper, settle it into position and really flatten the piece before you move onto the next stage.

Bias binding can be used to neaten seams or hems, to trim edges, and can be made into ties. Cut on the bias, its natural stretch means that it happily goes around corners, neatly lying flat, and for this reason, it is often used to trim necklines. It can be bought ready cut and folded, in myriad colors and widths, but making your own is a useful skill. The key is to make sure the fabric is cut at a perfect 45-degree angle to the selvage to even widths along its length.

MAKING BIAS BINDING

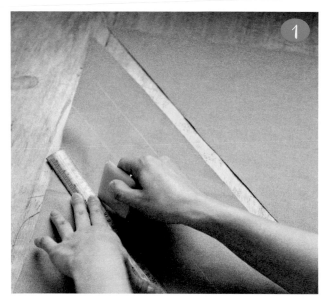

1 The 45-degree line is not difficult to manage. Simply pull out a thread running between the selvages and cut along the line it creates. Now fold this down until it matches the selvage. Press hard on the fold to create a crease, as this will be the first 45-degree line. Cut along the creased fold. Then, using a ruler, measure out the desired width of the bias—a useful standard is 2½" (6 cm) wide—at regular intervals along the length of the crease and draw in the first line parallel to the creased fold. Repeat several times until you have measured out enough length of bias for your desired project. Cut out the lengths of bias as accurately as you can. Scissors are fine, but you may find you can get more accurate cuts using a quilter's rotary cutter and ruler.

2 Now the lengths need to be stitched together. As they have been cut on the bias along the full length of the fabric, each one will have a 45-degree end. Place two pieces right sides together so that the long edges meet, creating a V-shape with little points at the end. Pin. Open out the piece to check you now have a long, straight piece of bias. If you don't, you've matched up the pieces wrongly—so try again! Once you are satisfied the pieces are pinned together properly, stitch. Snip off the points.

3 Press the seams open, then press the raw edges to the middle all along the length of the bias.

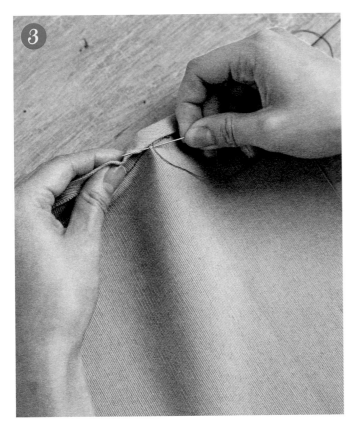

1 With right sides together, match one long
   raw edge of the bias binding with the edge to
be bound. Pin in position, placing the pins at right
angles to the raw edges. Stitch in the fold along the
length of the bias, then remove the pins.

2 Now trim the seam close to the line of
   stitching and turn the bias binding to the
wrong side along the stitching line, with the raw
edge folded under along the creased line.

3 Hand stitch the bias to the wrong side using
   slipstitch. Alternatively, turn the bias to
the wrong side, baste it over the original line of
stitching, then machine it in position, keeping as
close as possible to the folded edge. This is trickier
than hand stitching; unless you're an accurate
machinist, you could end up with uneven stitching.

Badly stitched buttonholes can ruin a garment and getting them right takes a lot of practice. Thankfully, nowadays even the most basic sewing machine has a buttonhole setting. Less sophisticated machines have one that involves four steps consisting of close zigzag stitches along the length of the buttonhole and a bar tack at each end. More sophisticated computerized machines have a special foot that can memorize the size of a button and then automatically stitch the right-sized buttonhole in one easy step. Practice several times on spare fabric until you are confident in your machining skills and sure the tension is absolutely correct. Make sure the test buttonholes are an accurate representation of the finished ones by using the same thread and layering up all the relevant fabrics, including facings, linings, and interfacings.

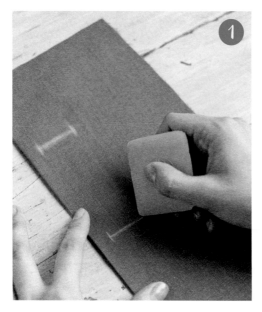

1 Start by marking the buttonhole positions. Many patterns have these printed in position and all you have to do is transfer the markings. If not, decide where the buttonholes should be. Measure out the positions carefully from the sewn edge to either end of each buttonhole and measure the distance from the hem upward to each end to make sure they are straight, evenly placed, and correctly positioned. Mark using tailor's chalk. Check the length of the buttonhole by placing the button on top of the mark. It should be fractionally longer than the diameter of the button— by the same amount as the depth of the button.

2 If you are making a four-step buttonhole, set the machine at the first buttonhole position and stitch along the top of the buttonhole. Adjust the dial to stitch the end bar. Adjust it again to stitch along the lower edge of the buttonhole, and finally, adjust for the other end bar. Place a pin at either end of the buttonhole just inside the end bars and snip between the pins using sharp embroidery scissors.

ADDING BUTTONS

1   Mark the button positions to correspond
with the positions of the buttonholes,
carefully measuring in the same way as you did for
the buttonholes. Mark with tailor's chalk.

2   Hold the button in position and, using double
thread knotted at the end, bring the needle
up from under the fabric through the first hole in
the button. Provide a little slack in the stitches by
putting a bobby pin or match across the button and
sew over it into the next hole. Continue in this way,
making a cross of stitches if it's a four-hole button.

3   Remove the bobby pin or match and create a
thread stalk by winding the thread between
the button and the fabric. Finally, pass the needle
through to the wrong side and make a series of tiny
stitches on top of each other at the back to secure.

SEWING GLOSSARY

BASTING Long temporary hand stitches used to hold pieces of fabric together before and during the machine stitching or final stitching step.

BIAS On fabric, this runs diagonally across the grain at 45 degrees to the selvage. This is where you can get most stretch out of the fabric. See also **GRAIN**.

BIAS BINDING Binding that is made from fabric cut on the bias.

BODICE The top part of a dress from the neckline to where it is sewn into the skirt.

CASING A channel created for threading through elastic or cord when making drawstring items.

DART A fold (often triangular or diamond-shaped) sewn into the cut-out fabric to give the garment a three-dimensional shape to fit the contours of the body.

FACINGS These are small pieces, cut to the same shape as an edge such as a neckline. Once sewn in position, they are folded to the inside to create a neat outside edge.

FEED DOGS See **THROAT PLATE**.

FINISHING Ways of neatening the raw edges of seam allowances (pages 50–51).

FRAYING The unraveling of the raw edges of the fabric.

GRAIN The threads in the fabric running either horizontally or vertically. Straight of grain, or lengthwise grain, runs parallel with the selvage and does not have any stretch. Cross grain or crosswise grain, runs between the selvages and stretches slightly, but is also a "straight grain."

GUSSET A piece of fabric used to create the three-dimensional element of some items such as the sides and bottom of a bag, the crotch of underwear, or even a small triangle of fabric at the end of a shirt seam.

HEM A neat finish whereby raw edges are turned to the inside of the garment. A double hem is folded over twice to enclose the raw edge on the inside before sewing, eliminating any fraying or unraveling.

INTERFACING Fabric used between the main garment piece and the facing to provide stabilization and extra body to the garment. Cut to the same size and shape as the facing, these were traditionally basted in place. Nowadays, specialized interfacings can be fused in position using a hot iron.

INTERLINING A layer between the main fabric and lining used to add body and/or warmth.

NAP This is the pile element on fabrics such as velvet, corduroy, velour, and velveteen that is woven into the material during the construction process.

PINTUCKS Tiny tucks, often stitched in parallel groups used to add detail.

RAW EDGES Any fabric edge other than a selvage.

RIGHT SIDES TOGETHER When sewing seams, fabric is placed so that the right side of the front piece is laid on top of the right side of the back piece with the shapes matching ready for sewing.

SELVAGES These are the finished edges running down either side of the fabric. They do not fray or unravel.

STAYSTITCHING Straight machine stitching worked just inside a seam allowance to strengthen it and prevent it from stretching or breaking.

THROAT PLATE The metal plate on the sewing machine underneath the needle and presser foot. It incorporates a hole for the needle and the feed dogs, which are metal teeth-like ridges that move the fabric forward as you sew.

TOPSTITCHING A line of stitches used decoratively to finish off the outside of a seam.

WRONG SIDES TOGETHER This is the term used when the wrong side of one piece is laid on top of the wrong side of another piece before sewing.

YOKE This is an extra piece of fabric at the top of a shirt or skirt to create an extra design element or extra strength. It is sometimes cut on the bias to emphasize the design.

FABRIC DICTIONARY

ACETATE
A silky synthetic fabric with excellent draping qualities. Most commonly used for garment linings.

BATIK
Printed cotton designs indigenous to Indonesia and Java. Wax is applied to the parts of the fabric that are to be left uncolored. The fabric is then dyed and once fully dried, boiled to remove the wax.

BOUCLÉ
A wool fabric incorporating loops and curls for a "poodle" effect.

BROCADE
Patterned fabric with the design incorporated into the weave. An extra horizontal thread is carried across the wrong side, which means the fabric is not reversible in contrast to damask, which is similar but fully reversible.

CALICO
Inexpensive, plain-woven, unbleached cotton fabric. Available in its natural state, it was previously offered as brightly patterned fabric known as calico prints.

CANVAS
A firmly woven heavyweight cotton.

CASHMERE
An expensive wool fiber made from Kashmiri goat hair. Very fine, soft, and warm.

CHALLIS
This is a soft, lightweight, often printed, fabric, traditionally woven from wool.

CHAMBRAY
A soft cotton fabric where the vertical threads are colored and the horizontal, white.

CHIFFON
This fine, sheer fabric was traditionally made from silk. Nowadays, you also see synthetic chiffon.

CHINO
A twill-woven cotton that has been "mercerized" to increase its strength and luster.

CHINTZ
A crisp, densely woven glazed cotton. Traditionally, it was printed (hence the word, chintzy).

CORDUROY
A cotton fabric featuring cut pile ridges. Available in several sizes from fine (needle) to large (elephant).

COTTON DUCK
Canvaslike cotton, woven using a horizontal thread over and under pairs of vertical threads. It comes in twelve weights ranging from the heaviest, Number 1 (18 oz) for hammocks, to Number 12 (7 oz), for lightweight clothes.

CREPE
Any fabric that incorporates twisted fibers to give a crinkled surface and improve drape.

CREPE DE CHINE
This is a silky crepe fabric where both vertical and horizontal threads are twisted before weaving.

DAMASK
A rich pattern-woven fabric similar to brocade. The difference is that damask is fully reversible.

DENIM
Robust cotton originating from Nimes in France (de Nimes, shortened to denim). The traditionally blue vertical threads are twill woven with white horizontals.

DOBBY
Fabrics featuring all-over woven repeats, which can take the form of a texture or a colored pattern. They're woven using a special head on a Jacquard-type loom.

DOGTOOTH CHECK
A pointed, star-like twill weave design using two contrasting colors. Larger versions are called houndstooth and smaller ones, puppy tooth.

DUPPIONI
A dense, slubby (nubby) silk fabric woven from fibers reeled off two cocoons. Synthetic versions, woven from synthetic slubby yarns, are now available.

ELASTANE
The generic name for Lycra.

FABRIC DYED
Fabric that has been woven, before being dyed, for a soft, washed, slightly faded look as the color doesn't penetrate the fibers so efficiently.

FLANNEL
A soft plain- or twill-woven cotton or wool.

GABARDINE
Tightly woven twill with a slight sheen.

GARMENT DYED
The fabric is dyed after the garment is made up for a washed look highlighting seams and turnings where the dye hasn't fully penetrated.

GEORGETTE
Similar to chiffon but heavier, this is a plain-weave crepe, traditionally made from silk.

GINGHAM
This firmly woven cotton is best known for its characteristic woven checked design in different sizes.

GROSGRAIN
A ribbon with distinctive ribs. Strong cotton horizontal threads are woven through fine silk or rayon.

IKAT
An ancient decorative fabric form with distinctive designs created by tying fibers into bundles using waxed threads so they can be part dyed before weaving.

INTERLOCK
A fine cotton knit traditionally used for underwear, this is now also used for outerwear.

JACQUARD
An elaborate loom invented in 1802 by Joseph Marie Jacquard to mechanize the production of brocades and damasks. Since its invention, any pattern-woven fabric or ribbon is generally referred to as "a Jacquard."

JERSEY
The name for knitted fabrics. T-shirt material is made from cotton jersey.

KNITTED FABRICS
All jerseys are created using a form of knit. This produces a soft, fluid fabric with plenty of stretch, even if it's made totally of natural fibers.

LAMÉ
Any fabric woven through with metallic threads.

LYCRA
A brand name for spandex, an extremely stretchy fiber.

MADRAS
A plain-woven, lightweight cotton from India that is characterized by striped and checked designs.

MOIRÉ
A watery effect created on ribbed fabric using steam, heat, and chemicals.

NYLON
The trade name for polyamide, an original synthetic fabric. It's mixed with other fibers for added strength.

ORGANDY
This sheer cotton fabric has a crisp quality that survives laundering, created by tightly twisting the yarns before weaving them together.

ORGANZA A silk organdy. Often made from soft, sheer synthetics, which lack the characteristic crisp drape.

OXFORD
A cotton basket-weave fabric, created by using two horizontal threads to weave under and over the verticals two at a time. Often used for casual shirts.

PAISLEY
A curved, teardrop-style motif native to the Indian sub-continent. It is named after the Scottish town of Paisley, where it is printed onto fine wool (challis).

PIQUE
This dobby woven cotton with its raised geometric design is a popular choice for casual wear, because it is cool, comfortable, and resists creases.

POPLIN
A fine (usually) cotton weave with a subtle rib running across its width.

POLYESTER
A versatile synthetic, often used in combination with natural fabrics.

RAW SILK
Natural, undyed silk before the gum has been removed. When woven, it gives a slubbed effect.

RAYON
One of the first synthetic fibers, first produced in 1891 as an alternative to silk.

SATEEN
A variation of the satin weave, created by carrying the horizontal threads over several vertical threads and then under one, giving a softer sheen than satin.

SATIN WEAVE
To create a sheen on one side of the fabric, the horizontal threads (weft) go under several vertical threads (warp), and over just one, then under several again. It's most effective and easily created using long fibers that have their own sheen, such as silk, but any fiber can be woven into a satin weave.

SEERSUCKER
A finely woven partly crinkled cotton. The name comes from the Anglicized Hindustani word for milk and sugar, describing the smooth/crinkled texture.

SHANTUNG
Originally a slubbed (nubby) silk, it now also describes synthetic slubbed fabrics.

SHOT SILK
By weaving together horizontal (weft) threads of one color with vertical (warp) threads in a different color, the fabric takes on an iridescent effect.

SLUB
A slubbed yarn is uneven or nubby along its length. When woven, it creates a slubbed fabric.

SPANDEX
Also known as Elastane or Lycra, spandex is a supremely stretchy synthetic developed in the 1950s. Originally used for swimwear, it is now also mixed with natural fibers to keep the fabrics in shape.

TAFFETA
A crisp fabric with a slight sheen, made from silk, rayon, or nylon.

TAPESTRY
A heavy embroidered fabric in which the horizontal threads completely cover the vertical. When it is machine made, the pattern is woven in using extra horizontal threads in a similar way to brocade.

TARTAN
A range of twill-woven wool plaids from Scotland.

TICKING
A densely woven striped cotton twill originally designed for mattresses. The quality of the smartly striped cloth has made it a popular furnishing fabric.

TOILE DE JOUY
Originated from Jouy-en-Josas in the late eighteenth century, the printed designs on usually cream cotton depict delightful pastoral scenes.

TULLE
Machine-made fine netting that was originally silk, but is now more often polyester.

TUSSAH
Made from silk from abandoned cocoons of India's wild silk worms, this fiber has a natural slub.

TWEED
Slubby, flecked wool fabric.

TWILL
A robust weave with a diagonal "rib." The twill most of us know best is denim, though chinos, drill, tartan, houndstooth, and ticking are also examples of twill. Twill is created by weaving the horizontal threads (weft) over two vertical threads (warp) and under one. The resulting fabric is hard-wearing, naturally resists soiling, and has a wonderful drape. Herringbone is a variant.

VELOUR
A soft fabric with a short, thick (usually cotton) pile, although it can also be found in wool or mohair.

VELVET
This luxurious pile fabric was traditionally made from silk; nowadays, it is more likely to be synthetic.

VISCOSE
A type of rayon, a silky synthetic fiber.

VOILE
Made from twisted yarns woven in a plain weave, this is a crisp semi sheer.

WOOLEN
A bulky fabric made from wool that has been carded but not combed before being woven, so that it retains some of the characteristic shorter fibers.

WORSTED
A fine-quality wool fabric that has been both carded and combed before being spun into strong fine yarns and then closely woven for a smooth, crisp fabric.

INDEX

ACKNOWLEDGMENTS

LOVE PRODUCTIONS would like to thank all the team at Quadrille Publishing who have worked so hard to produce this book, Tessa Evelegh who has cleverly managed to capture the spirit of sewing and translate it to the page, and May Martin and Patrick Grant for their minute attention to detail.

TESSA EVELEGH would like to thank the team that has put *The Sewing Bee* book together...

Stephanie Boissard for her inspired fashion designs and hard work to get everything done on time.

Jeanne Laine for her fabulous home furnishing and accessory designs, which are all so beautifully made.

Annie Kelley (Annie2Pins) for her brilliant stitching of the sewing skills.

Claire Louise Hardie (CL) for providing sewers at such short notice.

Lizzie Moul and her helpers, Francis Campbell and Maria Liljefors, for sewing a garments in a weekend.

Tilly Walnes of Tilly and the Buttons for generously sharing her pattern with us.

To all at *Love Productions*, including *Anna Beattie* for her unerring judgement on what is right, *Catherine Lewendon* for her sheer enthusiasm and getting me involved, *Letty Kavanagh* for her clarity and firm hand on the tiller, *May Martin* for checking the instructions and generally being lovely, *Patrick Grant* for his sheer style, *James Morgan* for his creativity and calm, *Jane Treasure* for supplying the stream of information needed for the book, *Susanne Rock* for her guidance, diplomacy, care, and attention to the book, and the production team, *Addy, Steve,* and *Sophie,* who looked after everyone's needs. *Stuart Cooper* at MetroStar for assembling the team.

To all at *Quadrille Publishing* including, *Jane O'Shea* for her wisdom, taste, and sharp eye for a deadline, *Claire Peters* for making the book beautiful, *Helen Lewis* for overseeing the look of the book, and *Lisa Pendreigh* for her cool-headed clarity in steering the book, and to *Sally Harding* and *Sarah Hoggett* for their dedication in editing all the instructions.

To the photography team, including *Laura Edwards* for her evocative photographs and *Jazmine Rocks* for her inspired, refreshing styling.

QUADRILLE PUBLISHING would like to thank the following:
Designers Guild, Kahaila Cafe, Labour and Wait, Malabar, Osborne & Little, Paul Johnston at *Fabrics Galore, Singer Sewing Machines, The Linen Works, Vanessa Arbuthnott, Warren and Sharon* at *Wimbledon Sewing Machine Shop, Tara Starlet, Bertie, Dune,* and *Pied a Terre.*

239

US version published by Fons & Porter Books, an imprint
of F+W Media, Inc., 10151 Carver Road, Suite 200, Blue
Ash OHIO 45252. Tel: (800) 289-0963. First Edition.

ⓕⓦ www.fwmedia.com

18 17 16 15 14   5 4 3 2 1

SRN: T4096
ISBN-13: 978-1-4402-4269-4
ISBN-10: 1-4402-4269-0

Text © Love Productions 2013
Project designs © Love Productions 2013
with the exception of
pages 46–51: Mathilde Blouse © Tilly Walnes
pages 68–75: Simplicity 2886 © Simplicity Ltd.
pages 126–133: New Look 6035 © Simplicity Ltd.

Photography © Laura Edwards 2013
Design, illustrations and layout © Quadrille Publishing
Ltd. 2013

This edition first published in 2013 by
Quadrille Publishing Ltd.
Alhambra House, 27–31 Charing Cross Road,
London WC2H 0LS
www.quadrille.co.uk

Distributed in Canada by Fraser Direct
100 Armstrong Avenue, Georgestown, ON,
Canada L7G 5S4
Tel: (905) 877-441.

Publishing Director Jane O'Shea
Commissioning Editor Lisa Pendreigh
Copy Editors Sally Harding and Sarah Hoggett
Assistant Editor Romilly Morgan
Creative Director Helen Lewis
Art Direction & Design Claire Peters
Assistant Designers Nicola Ellis, Gemma Hogan,
    and Katherine Keeble
Photographer Laura Edwards
Stylist Jazmine Rocks
Assistant Stylists Marianna Frannais
    and Becky O'Riordan
Hair & Make-up Danielle Hooker
Models Iskra and Quita at Hughes, Josephine at BMA,
    Sarah at Close, Tony at M&P, Honey at Bruce & Brown
Hand model Chinh Hoang
Illustrators Bridget Bodoano, Joy FitzSimmons,
    and Claire Peters
Production Director Vincent Smith
Production Controller Sasha Taylor